MW01258940

Are You Mad at Me?

Are You Mad at Me?

How to Stop Focusing
on What Others Think
and Start Living for You

Meg Josephson, LCSW

G

GALLERY BOOKS

NEW YORK   AMSTERDAM/ANTWERP   LONDON
TORONTO   SYDNEY/MELBOURNE   NEW DELHI

Gallery Books

An Imprint of Simon & Schuster, LLC

1230 Avenue of the Americas

New York, NY 10020

First Gallery Books hardcover edition August 2025

GALLERY BOOKS and colophon are registered trademarks of Simon & Schuster, LLC

Interior design by Matthew Ryan

Manufactured in the United States of America

1 3 5 7 9 10 8 6 4 2

Library of Congress Cataloging-in-Publication Data is available.

ISBN 978-1-6680-8246-1

ISBN 978-1-6680-8248-5 (ebook)

For those who have kept the peace
but lost themselves

Contents

Author's Note

As a therapist, protecting my clients and honoring the intimacy of the therapeutic relationship is my greatest priority. In these pages, I've created vignettes of individuals who reflect not actual clients but my experiences with them.

The stories contained herein are not about specific individuals but are a tapestry of shared experiences, inspired by the complexities of relationships, the impact of complex trauma, and the universal longing for connection and healing. My highest intention is to honor the stories and emotions of many while preserving the anonymity of all.

Are
You Mad
at Me?

Introduction

"Why do I *always* think people are mad at me?" I ask my therapist.

It's our first session together on a sticky, hot day in New York City. Her sage-green office is tucked between Union Square and Chelsea, and the shrill sound of passing sirens drifts into the room like a breeze. I'm twenty years old, interning at a lifestyle magazine for the summer in between my sophomore and junior years of college. I've saved up enough money to afford five to seven sessions with her over the summer, so I say a silent prayer to no one that she'll fix me up quickly.

In response to my initial question, she nods slowly and breathes deeply, waiting for me to say more while I wait for her to say anything. She adjusts her rectangular red-framed glasses and recrosses her legs, and my gaze settles on the painting above her chair. I squint my eyes and tilt my head as I try to decide whether it's a painting of a flower or a vagina.

At the end of our fifty minutes together, after providing her with some background on my life thus far, I walk out of her office with tearstained cheeks and a recommendation for a book on adult daughters of an alcoholic parent. *Weird, but okay.*

I had hoped that said therapist would tell me what was "wrong" with me and provide me with a three-step solution, a goodie bag, and a 2.0 version of myself. Instead, she spent most of the session asking me about my childhood, and in our subsequent sessions together I was gently brought to the realization that while I was no longer living at home, in some ways it felt like I was still there. I was no longer anticipating my dad's mood swings, but I was now anticipating getting fired anytime my boss messaged me. I was no longer analyzing the cadence of my dad's speech to see if he had been drinking, but I was now analyzing what it could mean when my friend texted with a period at the end of the sentence instead of an exclamation point. I no longer needed to be "perfect" and "good" to keep the peace at home, but I realized that I still felt terrified to be seen as anything *but* perfect and good now.

This hypervigilance—this unconscious sense of constantly being on high alert, on guard—was the thread weaving through both my childhood and my adulthood. It was during this summer that I finally understood that my present-day fears were not just phobias to overcome; in fact, they served a crucial purpose: they had kept my past self safe. What I viewed as self-sabotage had been self-protection.

After that summer I was confronted with the understanding that perhaps healing isn't a checkbox item but an uncomfortable, messy process of looking inward. *Huh.* But I was motivated. If there was one thing I was sure of, it was that I didn't want to live in a state of deep fear anymore. I felt like I was split in two: the younger part of me that was living in fear, and the wiser "parent" part of me that knew a better, more peaceful existence was possible. I just didn't know where to start.

So many people, especially women, struggle constantly with the notion that people are mad at them. We fearfully say, "Are you mad at me?" to our partners when they're in a bad mood, to our best friends when they don't text back, to our colleagues who didn't say hi to us when we passed each other walking out of the bathroom. Or maybe we *don't* ask and instead just silently ruminate about it when we're in the shower until our hands are pruney and when we're lying alert in bed at one a.m., chest tight, until we're too exhausted to think about it anymore.

Today, it may seem odd that we worry so much about how others perceive us given that we're in constant communication with one another. But it's precisely because of this endless receiving and giving of external validation and reassurance—texting, hearting *others'* texts, liking their posts, FaceTiming, DMing videos—that we are sent into tailspins of insecurity. When our bodies are so used to that intense amount of communication and then it's reduced in any way, this can easily send the part of ourselves that is focused on survival into a spiral. There are so many ways to tell someone you're thinking of them, and because of that, there are also so many opportunities to feel forgotten.

When I went back to school that fall, I got a pretty bad concussion after a drunk guy at a Halloween party fell against me, knocking his forehead into mine with an (almost) impressive amount of momentum. Doctor's orders were to take time off from classes, not look at screens, and rest in the darkness as much as possible. Whether I realized it then or not, this abrupt pause propelled me into a meditation practice and a spiritual practice that put me on a path back toward myself. It was during these months of recovery that I was forced, whether by that guy's rock-hard forehead or by the universe, to stop numbing myself, stop drinking, stop distracting myself. I had to stay with the emotions, memories, and wounds that I had ignored for so long, that had been tucked away into little dusty corners of my body and mind.

This is where I'm supposed to tell you exactly how I "healed" in a neat, buttoned-up paragraph. But my emotional healing was slow and subtle, and it's still ongoing. As the years passed, I didn't even realize how much I had changed until I looked back and noticed how different I felt in situations that had used to spark so much tension. Five minutes of meditation had once felt like an eternity when I was agitated by the discomfort of my inner world. And then one day I realized that I could sit for an hour with genuine ease. One month of no drinking turned into seven years. Something that would've once sent me into an overthinking spiral now seemed less overwhelming. I was able to experience a challenging emotion, identify the emotion, and realize that I didn't have to change it; I just had to alter my reaction to it.

After college, I felt an undeniable pull to support other people in their healing, to integrate the denser, trauma-based work with mindfulness-based practices. I had seen firsthand the benefits of integrating those two worlds. I went on to graduate school at Columbia University, where I received my master's in social work with a concentration in clinical practice while continuing to deepen my spiritual practice and study Buddhism. When I finished my graduate program and started practicing as a full-time therapist, my caseload quickly filled up, mostly with women struggling with anxiety, relationships, life purpose, self-confidence—and, most of all, people-pleasing.

On a foggy Tuesday in San Francisco (life update: I had moved across the country), I had a session with a client who talked about how she would head home after a social event anxiously replaying in her mind all the cringey stuff she had said. She'd convince herself that everyone hated her while swallowing the urge to text her friend an apology for something that she couldn't even put her finger on.

"Why do I always think people are mad at me?"

Here I was, now in the therapist's seat, my twenty-year-old college self mirrored back at me, being asked the same question I had once posed to my first therapist.

Later that day, I posted a video on social media in which I said, "Hey, you are not in trouble; you're okay. They aren't secretly mad at you. Your mind is lying to you because it's scared. I know you may have this fear that you're secretly a bad person and it's just a matter of time before everyone finds out, but you're actually safe."

Within hours, it blew up across platforms on social media, with thousands of people commenting things like, "Okay, why am I crying?"; "This was . . . oddly specific but true"; and "Are you inside my mind right now?"

I continued to post videos about this topic, this *feeling*, and every time, without fail, they'd have the same resonance with folks around the globe—and I continued to see clients come into my office with the same inner experience that was so familiar to me on a visceral level.

And so I wrote this book because it's one that I once desperately needed and one that I believe many people need.

There are lots of books out there about people-pleasing and codependency, but what's often missing is the true root of these behaviors, what precedes the need to be a people pleaser and abandon ourselves in the first place, and the context of why we do it. People-pleasing is the behavior we engage in when we fear that we're disappointing someone, that we're in trouble, that we feel unsafe in some way. It's the behavior that falsely soothes the queasy feeling that we've done something wrong. We can't do the inner work if we can't even pay attention to what's going on internally because we're so focused on looking outward at other people's perceptions and reactions. This book speaks to the root of the pattern—the fawn response. That is where true healing takes place.

Women in particular are conditioned to overextend, overexplain, overapologize. We're caretakers. Nurturers. Peacekeepers. We're taught to be good girls, cool girls, to agree with everything and everyone, and to give Uncle Richard a big hug, for goodness' sake, even if he makes us wildly uncomfortable. We're taught to not be too much or want too much, so we learn to get used to being unsatisfied with our lives. We're taught to meet everyone else's needs before our own, and along the way we lose the opportunity to get to know who we really are, what we need, what we like and prefer.

This is especially true for people who grew up in dysfunctional, high-tension, high-conflict, or emotionally neglectful home environments where *Are they mad at me?* was the exact internal question that made them feel safe. There's this popular narrative that young people, especially millennials, love to blame their parents for every negative aspect of their existence. But this work isn't about blaming; it's about finally looking at wounds that have been begging to be acknowledged, understanding how past wounds are seeping into our present so that we can move forward with more acceptance.

I approach this book the same way that I approach my clinical work: by blending mindfulness, spirituality, attachment theory, and Internal Family Systems therapy—all through a trauma-informed lens. I pull from both Western and Eastern psychology and philosophy, specifically Buddhism, integrating the mind, body, and spirit.

Are You Mad at Me? is about holding ourselves with the degree of compassion that we've always wanted but thought we didn't deserve. It's about shedding the protective mechanisms that are keeping us stuck in the past and away from the present. It's about releasing the belief that we need to neglect ourselves for the comfort of other people. It's about removing the conditioning and the blockages that have disconnected us from the true essence of who we are and what we want in life. It's about cultivating a sense of internal safety so that when everything else seems to be chaotic and out of our control, we have a quiet place to come back to.

This isn't a quick fix, because we're not some piece of machinery that needs to be repaired, and I am not an all-knowing being who holds the secret to your healing. I hope these pages reveal what you've known all along but has been blocked by your pain and conditioning. Healing is an imperfect, lifelong practice of realizing that we were never "broken" to begin with. It's a dance of forgetting wisdom and remembering it, again and again. My greatest hope is that this book supports you in your remembering. If, by the last page, you understand your patterns more clearly and hold yourself with more compassion, I've done my job.

Because once we stop focusing so much on what others think, we can remember who we are.

CHAPTER

The Other F-Word

*What the fawn response is and
how it has protected you*

"You're So Sensitive"

Throughout my childhood, I was often told that I was too sensitive. I was hyper-attuned to what was happening around me. I felt deeply and cried easily, about both pain and beauty, and I didn't get why that was so wrong.

When I was nine years old, my mom, bless her heart, sat me down and said to me softly, "Honey, I think you're starting to experience bodily changes that are creating more . . . hormones. And maybe that's why you're so sensitive."

Oh, cool. I finally have an answer.

I went up to everyone I saw that day, hands on my hips, and proudly declared, "I have hormones!"

As I got older, I started to feel shame about my sensitivity, like it was an ugly, inconvenient disease. "You're so sensitive" is rarely said as a compliment. My views on sensitivity are different now: I see it as a subtle superpower that allows me to feel things deeply and to get a clear sense of what others may be feeling. What I now celebrate about sensitivity is also why it sucked when I was growing up: I could feel what others were feeling—or, rather, I could sense what others weren't allowing themselves to feel.

As I later went through my graduate program and learned the ins and outs of trauma and its impact on the body, I started to question: *Was I "too sensitive," or did I learn to be superalert to people's emotions and mood shifts because my dad's rage could flip on like a switch at any moment? Was I "too sensitive," or was I just feeling all the unaddressed pain and tension that existed within the walls of my home? Was I "too sensitive," or did I just know more than my parents thought I did?*

Was I "too sensitive," or was it a fawn response?

The Fawn Response

Our brains' primary job is to keep us safe, plain and simple. This animalistic, survivalist part of our brains has been there since the beginning, for two hundred million years and then some, and is solely focused on basic motives such as avoiding harm, staying fed, and having sex. It's also in charge of the responses we slip into when we *don't* feel safe. When our brains think there's a threat of some sort, whether that threat is real or perceived, our nervous systems have four responses to turn to: fight, flight, freeze, and fawn.

This book focuses on fawning, which is the least talked-about trauma response yet arguably the most common one. "Fawn response" became a term only in the past decade or so, coined by the psychotherapist Pete Walker in his 2013 book *Complex PTSD: From Surviving to Thriving.* The other three threat responses are a bit more recognized: the *fight* response is about being aggressive toward the threat to make it go away (e.g., yelling or beating it up). The *flight* response is about physically leaving the environment or relationship (e.g., running away or ghosting). The *freeze* response happens when we can't physically leave, so we do the second-best thing by mentally departing and blocking out what's going on (e.g., dissociating, numbing ourselves, constant daydreaming).

But the *fawn* response? Oooooooh, the fawn response is about becoming more appealing to the threat, being liked by the threat, satisfying the threat, being helpful and agreeable to the threat—so that you can feel safe. Fawning is unconsciously moving toward, instead of away from, threatening relationships and situations. It's overlooked in our society because it's so largely rewarded. We get promotions for being people pleasers. We're called selfless when we neglect ourselves. We receive affirmation when we anticipate the needs of others and abandon our own. For many people, particularly for many women, the fawn response is learned in childhood and then reinforced by society; we're taught that our main role in life is to please, appease, and sacrifice our needs for the comfort of other people. Fawning has been a tool for survival, an unconscious way to feel in control in a society that strips power from us.

These four responses are not fixed traits, nor are they our destiny. We can slip into any and all of them at different points in time based on what our survival brains and bodies think will be the most effective.

Fawning isn't a conscious choice; it's a genius survival mechanism.

Walker explains that a fawn response develops in chaotic home environments when a child learns that the fight response escalates the situation or abuse, the freeze response doesn't offer much safety, and flight isn't always a feasible option. So, as an alternative survival strategy, the child "learns to fawn [their] way into the relative safety of becoming helpful."[1] All these stress responses are useful, adaptive, and necessary—but we're supposed to be in them for only a few minutes or hours at a time, not for years on end. Yet for so many, a chronic fawn response is as natural as breathing.

For most of my life, I thought fawning was just my personality. I almost took pride in it, thinking I was simply a cool girl who didn't have many preferences or opinions. I could be a chameleon in social circles that I didn't even want to be a part of and adjust my personality to be palatable to whomever I was trying to please.

That chameleon–cool-girl vibe was genuinely protective for a long time. I'd closely monitor my dad's moods and say the right thing at the right time, or not say anything at the wrong time. When I noticed my dad's behavior start to escalate, I did anything I could to prevent an explosive outburst. Honestly, it was just *easier* to make sure he was happy than deal with what would happen if he wasn't.

Maybe if I'm happy and perfect and good, he'll be happy, too. Maybe if I'm likable, he won't get upset at me. None of this was conscious, deliberate thought—fawning is an unconscious response.

Yes, fawning was protective for me then, but when I was past that time in my life, I was left feeling far from myself, like I hadn't yet met this person who was supposed to be "me." I'd look into people's eyes and think, *What do they want me to say?* And I'd say that.

I remember a seemingly small moment when I started to question whether this laissez-faire attitude was something less than positive, a sign that I had perhaps been neglecting myself. I was picking out bath towels for my first New York City apartment (read: shoebox), standing idly in aisle eight of Bed Bath & Beyond with no idea what to choose. I realized that I had zero clue what my favorite color was. My favorite color! I remember thinking, *Let me go on Instagram and see what other people like.* My next thought hit me like a punch to the gut: *Am I even real? Or am I just a medley of other people's personalities and preferences? Who am I when I'm not trying to please everyone else?*

Fawning Isn't Nice

As you start to become aware of the fawn response in your own life, you may be thinking, *When am I fawning, and when am I just being a nice person?* As humans, we're hardwired to connect. We're pro-social beings who naturally want harmony and belonging. Healing the fawn response does not push against that innate desire—it moves toward it. We can't be connected to others if we're not connected to ourselves.

With fawning, we have to abandon ourselves in order to make the appeasing possible. We learn that the other person's comfort is more important than our own, that we can't feel okay until the other person is okay. We learn that, in order for us to feel safe, we need to keep the peace, whatever it takes. And as a result, we're disconnected from questions such as *What do* I *need? What do* I *think? What do* I *want?*

What we'll come to understand together is the true difference between being nice and being compassionate. Nice is about how we're being perceived—it's doing something for the sake of being seen as good. Compassion is about authenticity, doing something because it *feels* good to be kind. It's not compassionate if we're constantly abandoning ourselves in our relationships. Being nice is often easier and a way to avoid conflict, but it can create long-term resentment if we're constantly sacrificing our needs to make someone else happy.

Motivation matters. *Why am I doing this? Am I saying yes because I want to or because I'm scared this person will be upset if I say no? Am I complimenting this person because I mean it or because I'm trying to make them like me?* When we can pause before engaging in habitual behavior, we can get clear on the motivation behind it.

Hypervigilance

A key component of fawning is something called *hypervigilance*, which is a state of heightened awareness in which the nervous system is extremely alert to potential danger or threat—whether there's an actual threat or not. In this state of alertness, the brain is continuously scanning the environment to find the threat. It's normal to experience brief moments of hypervigilance: like when you're trying to fall asleep and then you hear a weird noise down-stairs, your heart starts pounding, and you begin mentally mapping out an escape route to save your dear life—and then you realize the weird noise is just your dryer. *Hypervigilance complete.*

But for chronic fawners, that feeling of alertness is a daily occurrence, and it's exhausting. Anything and everything feels like a threat to the body. This hypervigilance carries over into *emotional monitoring*, which means we're constantly scanning other people's emotional states to gauge what they may be feeling so that we can adapt. Again, this occurs naturally through a part of our brains and is highly useful. But for those stuck in the fawn response, hyper-vigilance is on overdrive and happening when we're actually safe, leading us to analyze, ruminate, and worry: *Are you mad at me?*

The Hypervigilant Brain and Body

Enter the "new" brain. It's the part of our brains that makes us uniquely human and it has evolved over time to develop new abilities, like planning, analyzing, reflecting, imagining—and, in the case of fawning, ruminating for days on why your friends, who clearly saw your Instagram story, haven't responded to your text. To showcase how the human brain is so tricky, let's use one of my favorite visuals from the psychologist Paul Gilbert, founder of Compassion-Focused Therapy (CFT). First up, the animal brain:

A zebra is chomping on grass, basking in the sun and enjoying his delicious lunch. He then sees a lion out of the corner of his eye. His blood starts pumping and his heart starts thumping, ready to make the next move for his survival. *Okay, here we go.* In a split second, the zebra will make a decision. He's going to charge in the other direction, in one, two . . .

And then the lion saunters away, distracted by his next victim. *Phew.* The zebra immediately begins to calm down. The threat is gone. His nervous system is back to a normal, regulated state. Life is good. Back to eating grass.

Oh, to be a zebra.

For humans, life isn't as simple. We have the same survival instincts as zebras, but thanks to the new brain, we also have the ability to replay things in our heads, overanalyze, and fixate. So while a zebra will immediately go back to an internal feeling of safety once the threat is no longer present, a human has the ability to replay what just happened a million times in their head and think, *What if the lion comes back? What if the lion has a master plan to attack me in my sleep? Is the lion mad at me? Was it something I said?*

This means that our bodies can stay in that state of hypervigilance they entered when the lion was right in front of us. As humans, we can slip into survival mode whether the threat is real, remembered, or perceived.[2] We can have a threat response when we're actually safe—and we can stay in it for years, decades, a lifetime.

Anxiety is like an alarm system in that sense. Your body has wisely learned to look out for certain cues that set off the alarm (e.g., mood changes, body language), and when it notices them, the alarm starts blaring whether or not the threat is there. Even when you're perfectly safe, your body is physiologically responding as if you're in danger, waiting for the lion to pounce.

Does This Count as Trauma?

Isabelle, forty-three years old, sits across from me and reaches her arm out for another tissue to add to the growing pile on her left. It's our fifth session together, and she's telling me how, from the outside, it appeared that she grew up in a supportive home with the whole shebang: two parents married to each other, an older brother, a younger sister, and a fluffy dog that barked way too loudly for his size. But behind closed doors, her parents argued constantly; the air was always tense. Most of Isabelle's childhood memories are of being alone, hiding in the pages of a fantasy book borrowed from the library, left to soothe herself in the hope that her parents would make up by the time she got to the acknowledgments section.

She's been a self-described people pleaser her whole life, with a deep, dreadful feeling that something is wrong with her.

"I know this sounds horrible, but sometimes I wish something 'big' had happened to me, so at least then I could feel like I had a 'real' reason to feel this way. Then maybe people would believe me, and I'd believe myself."

This is a common feeling among clients when I explain that fawning is one of the four trauma responses. The word "trauma" tends to throw people off: "But doesn't trauma have to be this, like, one *big* event?"

Trauma can be an accumulation of "small," everyday moments that don't feel so small to the body.

Trauma is about how the nervous system perceives the event or period of time, how the body processes it. (This is why two siblings can experience the same thing and one can feel traumatized from it, while the other is unfazed.)

Trauma is what happens internally as a result of what happened to you. It's the wound that's hurting inside of you because of what happened—like the feeling of abandonment, the belief that you're unlovable, the fear of letting people in—and these wounds can form from a vast array of experiences, not just the "big" events that we often think of or see in mainstream media. The compounding nature of repeated "small" traumas can make them just as distressing and impactful as one "big" trauma.

When we're often left to feel unsafe, unheard, unloved, or unseen by those who are supposed to make us feel safe, the effect is called *complex trauma*. So often, complex trauma happens within the home or the caregiving system, because those are environments that are supposed to be sources of safety and stability.

Fawning is commonly born from environments where there was ongoing relational complex trauma—where the very relationships that should have felt nurturing and supportive didn't. This kind of trauma can occur in many ways, whether emotional, verbal, physical, sexual, or neglectful. Since complex trauma often derives from prolonged exposure to these events, it can be confusing to process, because for so long it just felt "normal." It was all you knew.

Complex trauma also involves what didn't happen, the support and nurturing that you didn't receive in the midst of the traumatic situation or in the aftermath. Did you receive the care that you needed, or were you left alone and told to "get over it"? What happens after the stressful event or incident deeply affects the way it's processed in the body. Because trauma is more about the wound and less about the event, healing is always possible. We can't reverse our history or change our past external circumstances, but we can always shift our internal experience.

Sometimes You Need to Fawn

Sometimes we have to fawn, whether it's to ensure our safety or to receive a paycheck. We can't talk about fawning as a survival response without also acknowledging the outside world and the systems we're living in. Because what is a fawn response if not an unconscious attempt to fit the mold of what our patriarchal, white-dominant society has decided is "good"?

Fawning has been necessary for women to survive in a culture dominated by men. Women have needed to please and appease men in the home, in the workplace, and in the world, both in public and in private. It wasn't even until 1974 that women were allowed to apply for and own a credit card under their name; how could women have survived in society *without* being attuned to male approval? On top of needing to do so for basic survival, women have been socialized to fawn. Feeling angry means you're crazy. Disagreeing means you're difficult. Being firm means you're a bitch.

Fawning has been necessary for People of Color (POC) to survive in a society where white people have long been the gatekeepers determining whether and where POC can acquire property, attend schools, get jobs, be paid, get promoted, or merely exist. "The most common manifestation of the fawn response among POC is probably the internalization of the model minority narrative, which appears to be universally pervasive among all POC communities. This narrative involves assimilating and complying with the rules set by dominant white culture to such a degree that white gatekeepers don't see the non-white person as a threat and may even view that person as an 'honorary' white person, so long as they reflect back to white gatekeepers their notion of a 'good Black person,' a 'good Asian person,' a 'good Mexican person,' a 'good Native American,' etc."[3] For people who are part of the LGBTQIA+ population, fawning is a common safety strategy.

My client Peter, who grew up as a closeted gay man in a strictly religious Catholic household, had to be highly aware of what others were doing, saying, and wearing so that he could adjust himself to fit the heteronormative majority. He played football through high school even though he would have preferred to take film classes. He paid attention to how others talked about women, and he dated women himself so that people would think he was straight. All we ever want, at any age, is to maximize our feelings of having others' approval and minimize our feelings of being rejected. When reflecting on that confusing time in his early life, Peter once said to me, "I'm so grateful that fawning exists, that my body knew to do that. I don't know if I could've survived it otherwise."

I've had clients who have struggled with disabilities, whether visible or invisible to others, who have come to acknowledge how necessary fawning has been for them to help them try to blend in with the majority: silencing their stutter, masking their neurodivergence in social settings, wearing a chunky sweater to conceal their spinal cord injury, depleting their energy just to keep up with their friends because they don't want to tell them about their chronic illness.

Your race, ethnicity, gender, sex, sexuality, class, cultural background, religious upbringing, and/or disability may feed into a fundamental need to fawn in order to live and survive within oppressive systems. Consider how the intersectionality of your various identities relates to your need to be seen as good, your fear of getting into trouble, your hypervigilance.

Remember: The fawn response is a necessary, adaptive mechanism for survival. Sometimes, we *do* need to fawn.

This work is about healing the fawn response in a way that's realistic and possible for you—shedding the fawn response when you don't need it, when you're actually safe.

REFLECTION QUESTIONS

1. In what ways do you notice yourself being hypervigiliant in your everyday life?

2. In what ways is it genuinely protecting you? Is it happening in areas where you may not actually need that hypervigilance?

It is safe to return
to myself now.

CHAPTER

2

Now
&
Then

*Case studies: How fawning
manifests and persists*

Be a Good Girl

We're squished into our 2001 Mitsubishi Mirage, which seats four people comfortably, or five people plus two dogs less comfortably. My parents are up front. I'm sitting between my brothers in the back seat, our shoulders and elbows mashing together, our two dogs laid out on our laps like blankets. I'm nine years old and we're on our first-ever spring break trip, from Minnesota to Florida— a twenty-one-hour drive, not including stops. It's a big deal, our first vacation together. My middle brother duct-taped a mini monitor screen onto the back of my mom's headrest so that he could plug his Xbox into it. My older brother is listening to his iPod, and my nose is buried in an American Girl book about puberty. I'm holding it close to my face so my brothers can't see the watercolor illustrations of what my boobs will eventually look like.

My mom and dad take turns driving, and right now it's my dad's turn. We were supposed to take exit 114, but my mom must have missed the cue because my dad starts yelling at her. He slams his foot on the gas, accelerating, because his anger has to be channeled somewhere. My eyes are ripped from the page about how to insert a tampon, and I flinch as my dad grabs the MapQuest directions from my mom's hands and tears them into a bunch of pieces. We all stare in silence because this is what he does sometimes, and it's easier to just be quiet.

"Calm down, it's fine," Mom whispers.

Eventually he does, and we pull over to the shoulder of the

highway so he can tape the map back together, because we need to get to Florida somehow. (GPS wasn't a thing yet.) We get back on track, cramped together in a tense silence that feels like a held breath, and one command rattles through my mind: *Be good.*

When I was growing up, I thought every kid learned to know their parents' moods by the sound of their footsteps on the stairs. I thought every household held addiction behind closed doors like a superstition, a secret you shouldn't talk about too loudly because words were spells and muttering its name could make it reappear. I thought everyone's dad had a temper that could rattle the glasses on the kitchen table, and then the next hour the parents would be chatting normally about what they should do for dinner. "Every family has its problems" was what everyone said, so maybe others had the same ones and ignored them the way we did.

When conflict is constantly brushed under the rug, though, the person who decides to lift up the rug and address the issues—the person who's healing—is naturally going to have a harder time believing their own experiences because no one else is there to say, "Yeah, that did happen, and what you're feeling makes sense." The child who's called "dramatic" is made to feel like they're the problem, but really, they're often just the one communicating the problem that others aren't willing to look at.

Before I went to that first therapist at age twenty, I was in denial—a season of refusing to admit that my early experiences had an impact on me. My story isn't special by any means, but I used that reasoning to deny that it was real. A lot of the turmoil that I remember happened in my teenage years, so I thought it didn't count. Wasn't I old enough to handle it by then? I thought that in order for my experience to be "bad enough" for me to be affected by it, it would have to have been *all* bad, *all* the time. It wasn't, and that was confusing. There was volatility and emotional neglect and addiction, but my dad painted my room pink for me the summer I turned twelve, and he let me wear his oversize flannel shirt to bed, and my parents would watch me perform Hannah Montana's "Nobody's Perfect" in our living room on a weekly basis—a cappella with choreography—applauding every time. Beginning my healing meant first releasing the black-and-white thinking that was keeping me from it. There can be parts that were loving and other parts that hurt, and the loving parts don't negate the reality of the hurtful parts and the hurtful parts don't negate the love.

The point of this work isn't to stay infinitely stuck in a place of blame and bitterness toward your parents or your past but to acknowledge and objectively understand how your early life experiences have affected you, so that you can begin to heal from them. The point is to finally allow yourself to acknowledge the emotions that others didn't. The point is to see that your parents' actions and reactions weren't your fault; they were reflections of your parents' own unprocessed pain—their own inner children who were aching. This certainly doesn't excuse any behavior, but it helps us to understand it.

After years of training as a therapist and working through my own struggles, I see now that my defensiveness at the time was coming from a place of self-protection. If I didn't admit that my early experiences hurt me, then maybe they didn't happen, and I wouldn't need to address the lingering pain and could continue to hold on to the image of my parents that I wished were true.

My next line of defense was "Yeah, but does it really matter? I turned out fine!"—and I did, in many ways. I had succeeded up until that point with all the checkboxes marked that a parent could hope for. I was a good girl with good grades at a good school; I had a shitty boyfriend here and there, but I was *good*. And yet, there was a deep part of me that didn't feel so good. Actually, there was an even deeper part of me that felt very bad, like *I* was bad.

I was an adult and I was still walking around with a constant feeling that I was about to get into trouble. I was an adult and I still assumed other people's bad moods were automatically my fault, and that I was personally responsible for managing and "fixing" their emotions.

Before I even graduated college, I promised myself I would never have a boss because of my self-declared entrepreneurial spirit, but the truth was, I was hiding behind my fears; I just wanted to eliminate any and all possibility that an authority figure could get mad at me. I was stuck in a fawn response.

Learning to fawn is *especially* necessary in certain childhood and adolescent dynamics where fawning is learned not just in society but within the four walls of a home that should have been a refuge, a place to put down the armor. Most people pleasers were "parent pleasers" first. The following are some client stories that explore common dynamics in which fawning is learned and the roles that each client learned to play as a child and continues to play as an adult.

You may see yourself in one of these vignettes, or maybe a nugget from each will resonate with you. There's no one-size-fits-all reason for fawning, because you have your own unique experiences, identities, and nervous system. What matters more is the *feeling* that weaves your past into the present, your current experience of neglecting yourself as an unconscious way of trying to protect yourself. Fawning looks different for everyone, but the fundamental feeling is there: *My safety comes from pleasing you. I can't feel safe until I know you like me.*

IF YOU GREW UP IN AN ENVIRONMENT WHERE . . .

. . . THERE WAS A LOT OF CONFLICT AND NO REPAIR

BRIANNA'S STORY | THE PEACEKEEPER

Brianna came from a close-knit family of four, but conflict at home came in two flavors: screaming matches and silent treatment. Her mom couldn't manage her own emotions, and her moods set the tone for the rest of the family. If she was happy, everyone else could exhale a sigh of relief and be happy, too. If she was in a bad mood, they needed to hold their breath and tiptoe around her. "Don't tell Mom" was often whispered between the walls—telling her was never worth the risk of upsetting her. This dynamic led Brianna to hide most things from her mom: who she was crushing on at school, a comment that a bully had made, her anxiety about her upcoming math test. Hiding these things was just easier. *Which mom will I get now?* Brianna wondered each morning, each hour.

For families like Brianna's, the family dynamic revolves around keeping the most dysregulated and dysfunctional person happy. Small things could set her mom off: a restaurant messing up her order, the dishwasher not being loaded properly, Brianna or her brother asking if friends could sleep over. While these things were trivial, Brianna's mom would react in a big way. She'd explode and slam doors, and once she cooled off—silence. Brianna's mom would stomp around the house, ignoring Brianna's pleas of "*Mom?* When are you going to talk to me?" Brianna would try to lock eyes with her even just for a second, but her mom would turn her back and walk away. One summer her mom didn't talk to her for an entire month for a reason Brianna can't even remember.

Stuck in the silence, Brianna felt confused and alone. She tried to make sense of her mom's reaction by unconsciously concluding that it was entirely her fault, that she was personally responsible for her mom's unhappiness, and that her mom's needs mattered more than her own. Eventually her mom would start talking to her again, but for only one of two reasons: either Brianna would softly knock on her mom's locked door and apologize for what she did wrong, even if she didn't know what she was apologizing for, or if that didn't work, the silence would end out of necessity, such as when they needed to discuss a form that had to be signed or the logistics of leaving for school. From this, Brianna learned that silence felt like abandonment. She learned, *When someone isn't responding to me, it's because I've done something terribly wrong. When someone is mad at me, I need to immediately apologize in order for things to get better.*

As a way to adapt, Brianna took on the **Peacekeeper** role. This was her safety strategy growing up, and it continues to be her role in her adult relationships. She constantly feels like a burden and downplays her issues out of fear of being considered too "dramatic" or "sensitive," because that's what she was told as a child whenever she expressed herself. She fears that she's secretly a bad person and that if anyone loves her, it's only because she's "fooled" them.

She learned that the best ways to prevent conflict are to go along with what everyone else wants and to overapologize when conflict does arise. She keeps the peace by staying out of things, remaining neutral, and seeing what others think before she decides what *she* thinks. She often has her head in the clouds, because it feels safe up there. She's seen as "soooo chill" in relationships, but she really just never got the opportunity to explore her own opinions and preferences. She's terrified of conflict—scared a disagreement will ruin the whole relationship because when she was growing up, conflict was such a big deal. She struggles with indecision as a result of not knowing what she truly wants and not wanting to piss anyone off.

Fawning is commonly birthed in environments like the one Brianna grew up in, where there was lots of conflict—in whatever form it took, whether screaming matches, silent treatment, or passive aggression—with little to no repair or acknowledgment after the fact. Conflict is inevitable (more on that in chapter 8), but a crucial component of conflict is the repair that follows it. Repair from a parent could sound like "Hey, I'm sorry for raising my voice at you. That was my fault, not yours, and I'm really working on managing my frustration" paired with the parent's active effort to self-soothe in the future.

So many of my clients who had emotionally immature parents express that the most painful part of childhood trauma wasn't the trauma itself but that it was never spoken about. And when they did want to talk about it, they were shut down, made to feel like they were making a big deal out of nothing, or were countered with responses that closed off any opportunity for conversation. For Brianna, this sounded like hearing, "I guess I'm just the worst mom ever!" and "I can't say anything right. I'll just keep my mouth shut." A child usually wants repair and is open to it—and so much healing can happen when a parent wants it, too. In fawn-ridden households, there's high conflict, which is buried after an incident, and then life continues as usual. Maybe the child is told that the parent's reaction is the child's own fault—"Look what you made Dad do!"—or the other parent forces a child to apologize to the volatile parent just to make the conflict go away. To the child, this is wildly confusing. When repair isn't made, accountability isn't taken, or conflict isn't acknowledged, self-blame—in which we believe *we* are responsible for the stressor's occurrence—becomes a natural coping mechanism.[1]

A child is left to make sense of the conflict on their own: *I made Dad upset; I must have done something bad.* When this happens again and again, the child's explanation evolves from *I cause bad things to happen* to *I **am** bad.* Because of this, it's normal for a fawner to carry a deep sense of shame and to fear that they're secretly a bad person, a fear that's held close, in silence. It's so much safer to believe that we're bad than to think that our parents can't take care of themselves and therefore maybe can't fully take care of us. We come to believe that something is truly, inherently wrong with us. This deep, chronic shame leaves us feeling unworthy, unlovable, and bad at the core.

The Peacekeeper believes:

- It's easier to shove my emotions down than to risk upsetting the other person.
- I need to prove to other people that I'm good because I fear that I'm bad.
- When people are in a bad mood, it's my fault.
- I shape-shift depending on what others are feeling.

. . . THERE WAS CONSTANT TENSION
THEO'S STORY | **THE PERFORMER**

"My parents were always snapping at each other passive-aggressively. It was like their main communication style was just bickering," Theo told me. There wasn't much conflict at all because things were never brought to the surface. Instead, there was constant tension that was more felt than spoken; Theo felt it in the air he breathed. He was an only child, so maintaining harmony in his parents' relationship was his main focus. His parents were unhappily married; he knew that much. Years of resentment lingered over their home like a thick cloud, to the point where he didn't think even they knew why they were so unhappy anymore. He'd gather hints of where the resentment came from, hearing comments like, "Good to know Theo has *one* responsible parent" and "Oh, don't worry, I can handle everything, as usual." He knew that his dad was always out of work. He knew that money was a constant worry—that there was never enough of it. And as he got older, he knew that both of his parents were severely depressed.

He'd watch as his parents exchanged passive-aggressive remarks, and he'd try to mediate, crack a joke, divert the conversation, so that the tension could be dissolved. He told me, "I know this might sound weird or bad, but I remember secretly wishing they would divorce. So then at least the tension would be over, they could be happy, and I could be free."

A tense home is the birthplace of hypervigilance.

Even if the tension isn't directed at you, it's the environment you're stuck in. In a high-tension environment, the child is constantly focusing on other family members' moods and always trying to correct course. *Mom seems hurt—I need to soothe her so Dad doesn't get annoyed that she's upset. Dad seems like he's getting mad—I need to divert the conversation so that he switches back into a good mood.* This can also be true for children of a single caregiver who struggles to manage and regulate their own emotions. The child thinks: *How can I make my parent happy, and what am I doing that's making them unhappy?*

For Theo, this looked like being the **Performer**, using humor and relentless positivity as strategies to ward off his parents', especially his mom's, tension and depression. He just wanted her to feel better. As an adult, he thinks he's responsible for making people feel happy and struggles to be "himself" because it's like he's always onstage. Because of this, he has a hard time letting people get to know him beneath the surface.

It's both lonely and exhausting to live this way. He's sent into an anxiety spiral anytime he thinks someone's in a bad mood, and he wants to make sure everyone likes him. This makes sense. He learned that when someone's upset, he'd feel unsafe in some way, or he'd need to guess what they were feeling. Confrontation makes him uncomfortable because he never witnessed it being handled in a calm, productive way. He's constantly catastrophizing, pre-

39

paring for the worst-case scenario, because he never knew when things would switch from being good to being not so good. He's been conditioned to assume something is wrong when nothing's being said, so he's always reading between the lines and overthinking his every move in relationships.

The Performer believes:

- I'm personally responsible for making other people happy.
- I need to butter people up to make sure they like me.
- It's unsafe for me to relax.
- I'm always performing, and I need to "keep up" the version of myself that people expect me to be.

. . . YOU PLAYED A PARENTAL ROLE FROM A YOUNG AGE
SOPHIE'S STORY | **THE CARETAKER**

When Sophie was growing up, her younger sister struggled with severe learning disabilities that coincided with mental health issues. Her sister's moods were unpredictable, and most of her parents' time and energy went to tending to her sister's needs and making sure she was stable. All Sophie wanted was a peaceful home and a sliver of the care that her sister got, so she was left constantly asking herself: *How can I make my sister, and therefore my parents, happy?* Her parents would say "Let your sister choose" whenever they all watched a movie together, and their family outings would revolve around her sister's preferences. On the rare occasions when Sophie saw friends outside school, she'd often get a call saying, "We need you to come home and look after your sister. She's having a tough time." Sophie loved her sister and would have done anything for her—she just didn't realize how far she felt from herself in the process.

Sophie found safety by taking on the *Caretaker* role. All any child wants is to feel loved and safe, and Sophie found these feelings by being helpful. She was her parents' unofficial therapist, listening to them vent about each other, their day-to-day problems, their own mental health struggles, and the details of their own childhood traumas. She'd never talk about her own issues, not wanting to add to their responsibilities. She'd pick up any chore she could, hoping that by doing so she could free up some time her parents could spend with her.

She was always putting her sister's needs and preferences before her own, and this strategy was reinforced by her parents, who would say things like, "You're such a good girl," and "You're the glue of this family. What would we do without you?" Teachers often told Sophie, "You're so mature for your age!"—and she was, because she had no choice but to grow up quickly. She spent so much of her time and energy meeting her family's physical and emotional needs that she forgot she had needs of her own.

As an adult, Sophie overextends herself and then feels secretly resentful. She struggles to set boundaries and gets all her feeling of value from being nurturing and helpful. She was a *parentified child*—fulfilling part of the parent role from an early age. Sophie grew up to be a hyperindependent adult: she feels like she has to do everything on her own and struggles to ask for help. She's the therapist-friend, the person everyone goes to with their problems, but she feels like her problems and emotions are burdens. Sophie got the message that she could receive love and attention by alleviating other people's stress. But now when *she's* stressed or overwhelmed she feels like she needs to hide those feelings. No one ever thinks to check in on her because they assume she always is fine and has it together. She unconsciously seeks out romantic relationships in which she needs to mother her partner because that's the dynamic that feels familiar to her, but it leaves her resentful and exhausted.

As a parentified child, she developed a harsh inner critic, which has served as a necessary stand-in to give her the parenting and guidance she wasn't able to get while she was busy caring for everyone else. She also finds herself being critical of people who aren't as self-sufficient as she is, in part because she's envious that they didn't have to grow up so quickly.

Maybe you grew up with a single parent or had a parent or sibling with a disability or a severe mental health issue. Maybe you grew up with immigrant parents who relied on you to help them assimilate into the new culture. Maybe you experienced financial scarcity or just grew up with parents who couldn't emotionally fill the parental role. There are so many circumstances that create the role of the parentified child, and that role is always the same: in order for you to feel safe and secure, you had to put your needs aside from a very young age.

The Caretaker believes:

- I thought that if I cared enough for them, they'd eventually care about me.
- I need to manage other people's emotions so that I can feel okay.
- Other people's needs are more important than my own.
- My value is in being helpful and taking care of others.

. . . THERE WAS FREQUENT EMOTIONAL NEGLECT

ALICIA'S STORY | THE LONE WOLF

Growing up in a family of five, Alicia felt alone. Even when she was in the same room with her parents, they felt miles away, not showing interest in what was going on in her life, not putting in the effort to get to know who she was. She went to camp for a month, and she watched as her peers received care packages stuffed with their favorite candies and handwritten notes about how much their parents missed them. She never got a package and thought to herself, *I don't even think my parents know what my favorite candy is.*

It felt like the only ways for her to connect with her family were complaining and gossiping. She craved a deeper connection with her parents, but when she tried to talk about something real with them, they'd wave her off, poke fun at her, or change the subject. It's not that they were mean; they were just so focused on themselves, and she didn't have any extended family to connect with on a deeper level.

When Alicia was feeling distressed and seeking comfort, she'd have to find it on her own. After arguments with her parents, she'd cry in her room and secretly hope that they'd softly knock on her door and comfort her, but they never did. When she was sick, her parents viewed the illness as an inconvenience, as if getting sick were her active choice to make their lives worse. They viewed her emotional distress not as a bid for comfort or connection but as a burden, something to silence. That was all she had known, and it was what she thought was normal.

Like Sophie, Alicia grew up to be hyperindependent because she'd learned that it was unsafe to rely on other people for support. As an adult, she even finds herself unconsciously not wanting to tell her parents when things are going well in her life, because she fears that if they think she's doing fine, they will fully stop caring about her.

Emotional neglect can be so confusing to process because it's about what *didn't* happen. It's not necessarily something we can even point to; we just feel it and internalize it as *I'm not lovable, and if I want to be loved, I need to work really hard for it.* There aren't physical markings, such as negative feedback or criticism—emotional neglect just creates a feeling of loneliness, of not being seen or heard. This is especially true if you had a caregiver who wasn't emotionally involved, who was emotionally absent.

When a child's emotional needs are repeatedly unmet, they feel that they're not worthy of receiving love, that they need to earn approval from others, since it won't come naturally. With this belief there's a deep fear of rejection or abandonment, because the child has learned that their needs don't matter or are "too much."

To avoid that rejection and the pain that goes with it, they'll suppress their needs, brush them off, and constantly look externally for validation to boost their self-esteem.

Alicia found comfort by being a *Lone Wolf.* She learned to rely on herself not out of desire but out of necessity. She received the most praise from her parents when she wasn't "bothering" them. "You're so easy," they'd say, and that was how she made them happy. This Lone Wolf behavior seeped into all facets of her life: she played only individual sports (mainly tennis) so that she'd continue to be seen as succeeding on her own, without the support of others, and so she couldn't let anyone down. She never "bothered" her parents with anything, whether she was struggling with a homework assignment or experiencing crippling anxiety as a teenager. She felt safest alone in her room.

As an adult, Alicia isolates. Because she learned that her needs wouldn't be met, she doesn't want to burden anyone with hers, leading her to keep her distance in relationships. The closer people want to get to her, the more she fantasizes about being alone, because the possibility of having her needs seen and then rejected once again feels too painful. She's lonely but craves deep connection and will constantly look outward for approval and validation to soothe the part of her that wants to be seen.

The Lone Wolf believes:

- Love should feel really hard to get.
- I avoid conflict by never allowing myself to get close to people.
- It's unsafe to let people really get to know me.

Fawning and Attachment Styles

In terms of attachment styles, I've found that fawning is most commonly seen in people who resonate most with anxious-insecure attachment. But as we'll explore and as we can see from the preceding vignette, fawning is also protective for people who identify with avoidant-insecure attachment. In the same way that fawning isn't a fixed or static trait, neither are attachment styles. Whether we're coping with more anxious (e.g., seeking reassurance, ruminating, clinging) or more avoidant (e.g., self-sufficiency, hyper-independence) behavior, the underlying goal is the same: to prevent abandonment and rejection and to maximize feelings of safety and security in relationships. *How* we do that is based on what our bodies perceived was the safest, most effective thing to do in our early attachment experiences.

We can slowly learn to develop secure attachments in relationships even if we didn't witness them growing up. The same is true for fawning—we can learn to exit a chronic fawn response at any point in our lives. Regardless of your attachment style or how fawning manifests for you, the goal remains the same: to cultivate a sense of internal safety. When relationships fluctuate, body language shifts, or life throws stressors at you, you have a place of inner stability to return to and to consciously reconnect with yourself, your needs, your body, and your emotions.

. . . YOU WEREN'T ALLOWED TO FEEL CERTAIN EMOTIONS

CARTER'S STORY | **THE PERFECTIONIST**

As a first-generation immigrant daughter, Carter felt insurmountable pressure to be perfect and to make her parents proud. Her family was close and loving, but there was lots of emphasis on achievement and on how she and her family were perceived. Carter's dad was very critical, and being perfect was a way to get ahead of his criticism. Carter went to medical school right after college. This was not a decision she made but a decision that was made for her before she could even hold a pencil. Her parents often had difficulty regulating their own emotions, and Carter had to endure their outbursts—yet when she felt any sort of sadness, anger, or fear, her parents dismissed it, saying that it wasn't "productive." Consequently, Carter never learned how to *deal* with challenging emotions. She learned to believe that when she experienced such emotions—which she would, because she was a living, breathing human being—she needed to shove them down. And because any challenging emotion was discouraged or ridiculed by her parents, she learned to believe that something was wrong with her for having such emotions. This lack of validation and acknowledgment made Carter feel invisible and unsupported.

Carter adapted by taking on the ***Perfectionist*** role. She was the high achiever, the golden girl. She cried in middle school when she got an A on a history paper instead of an A+. She's a charmer who morphs her personality to match that of whomever she's with and wants to be liked by everyone—even if that means not always liking herself. She's terrified of making a mistake, and of having people finding out that she did, because when she was growing up she was heavily criticized whenever she made one, like when she accidentally broke a glass or missed the goal at soccer practice. She feels crippled by any sort of negative feedback because being seen as anything but perfect has felt entirely unsafe.

She needs people to think she's always productive, and if she hears someone walk through the door, she'll quickly swap the TV remote for a book so they don't think she was, gasp, relaxing. She's very hard on herself and never feels like she's doing enough; she walks around with a deep sense of shame for not being the perfect person she expects herself to be. She's scared to try new things and stays within her comfort zone because she's terrified of being a beginner. She often feels like she's putting up a front so people won't see the messiness underneath. As a result, she feels like people don't know the "real" her. She learned: *I need to be perfect to be loved.*

The foundation for our inner sense of security is the emotional connection that we have with our caretakers. If you were criticized or dismissed for expressing emotions and didn't have a caregiver who was there to help you work through them, you may have come to believe that there was something wrong with you but not understood what. When you're constantly told as a child things along the lines of "Don't cry!" "You're so dramatic!" "You're so sensitive!" or "What's wrong with you?" you end up feeling like something is wrong with you for having emotions that your parents can't hold.

The Perfectionist believes:
- My emotions are too much, and I'm never doing enough.
- I need to be 100 percent "on" in order for people to like me and not leave.
- I need to be perfect to be loved, so I'm constantly trying to impress other people.
- At my core, something is wrong with me.

. . . YOU EXPERIENCED BULLYING

RACHEL'S STORY | **THE CHAMELEON**

Rachel was bullied as a kid, especially in middle school, when she and her family had just moved from a different state. During the first week of school, the "cool" crowd made it their mission to pick on Rachel for entertainment, so they commented on her outfit choices and laughed at any contribution she made in class despite the teacher's warnings to stop. Rachel remembers a pivotal moment when said cool crowd invited her to eat with them at lunch. She was skeptical but hopeful as she grabbed her PB&J and chocolate milk and tiptoed to their table. When she went to take a seat, a boy pulled the chair out from under her and she fell to the floor.

The whole table erupted in laughter, and Rachel ran to a bathroom stall, where she burst into tears.

When she went home later that day, she was eager to tell her parents, in the hope that they'd comfort her. Instead, they smirked, held back laughter, and told her to toughen up. "I'm sure it's not as bad as you're making it out to be. Just try to fit in more," her dad said. The bullying continued, and her parents continued to dismiss it.

Something shifted in Rachel. She wasn't going to let the bullying persist. She adapted by playing the *Chameleon*. She started watching the shows that the cool crowd talked about, listening to the music they listened to, doing her hair the way they did theirs—not to be part of their crowd but so they wouldn't have anything to make fun of her for. This marked the birth of Rachel's fawn response, in order to avoid conflict and harm and maximize approval by morphing into someone the bullies wouldn't target.

As an adult, she feels far from herself, out of touch with her own desires, preferences, and personality. She feels empty and lost, uncertain about who she is and what she wants. She struggles to speak up for herself and finds herself adjusting her opinions to match those of whomever she's with, which leads to a large amount of self-loathing, thinking she's an impostor faking her way through the world. She's terrified of being seen, which leads her to hide her gifts and silence her dreams as a way to prevent herself from being perceived and then judged.

. . . YOU EXPERIENCED ABUSE

LUCY'S STORY | THE CHAMELEON

Like Rachel, Lucy found safety in being a Chameleon. During her early teenage years, her stepfather sexually abused her under their own roof, unbeknownst to her mom. When he went through seasons of being particularly unhappy—at work, with her mom, in general—the abuse increased. Scared and confused, she started to have thoughts of self-blame: *What would my mom think of me? Did I send the wrong signal? Did I cause this?*

During the horrific years of being isolated with this abuse, Lucy found safety by going along with whatever her stepfather wanted and asked for. *If I can just keep him happy, maybe the abuse will stop.* She tried to please him as best she could: being extra quiet, laughing at his jokes, cooking dinner for him and her mom most nights.

In our sessions together, Lucy would express the deep shame she felt about the abuse, fearing that she had been an active participant in what had happened. She had craved her stepfather's approval, she had appeased him to get it, and this led to self-loathing. Over time she came to recognize that because she had been abused by someone who was older, stronger, more powerful, and living in the same home, fawning had been her best strategy to reduce the immediate threat. Fighting back would've put her in danger. Leaving home hadn't been an option. How *brilliant* that her body knew to fawn.

51

—

Most of the case studies on abuse in this chapter have been about forms of emotional abuse and neglect that often go unnoticed. For people who have experienced *any* form of abuse—whether sexual, physical, emotional, or narcissistic—at *any* point in life, fawning is a common, brilliant, and underrecognized strategy. It doesn't have to look like being a chameleon—it can look like putting all your energy and attention into pleasing the abuser, spending more time with them, defending them, doing anything in your control to make them happy. This can include *sexual fawning*—complying with unwanted sexual advances or even initiating flirtatious or sexual encounters with someone who feels threatening. When others say, "Why didn't you just leave?" they don't understand the fawn response's role in surviving abuse.

Staying in an abusive or toxic relationship, even when there's a part of you that knows it's abusive or toxic, is often a fawn response hard at work.

Maybe if I can just make them happier, it'll be okay. If I can just be easier and more agreeable, maybe things will calm down. It's especially confusing when there are loving moments along with the abusive ones, because they lead you to unconsciously start to believe that you're causing the turmoil—that it's your fault. You grasp onto the loving moments even if they're mere breadcrumbs and think, *Maybe it's not so bad after all.* The core, unconscious motivation of fawning remains the same: *I can be safe only once I know that you're pleased with me.* It's common to feel shame and to get sucked into self-blame, but your body was brilliant in figuring out the best way it could to stay safe in the threatening situation you were in.

The Chameleon believes:

- I must blend in and make myself small to be safe.
- I'm not allowed to say no.
- I don't know who I am or what I want.
- Being seen or perceived is dangerous.

"BUT I DON'T REMEMBER MY CHILDHOOD"

I don't have many childhood memories, and the ones I do have are blurry, like flashes of movie scenes. In a lot of them, I'm existing in solitude, passing time by myself. Childhood memory is weird: even if you grew up in a safe, stable, and loving environment, you're not going to remember *all* of your childhood because your brain was still developing then. But if you experienced trauma, whether it was a big singular event or daily smaller events, your memory will be even spottier.

Research has shown that trauma leads our brains to block out memories, even whole periods of time, as a way to protect us from the emotional pain associated with those memories and times.[2] *Do I not remember because of that, or because I was just a kid?* It's confusing. When I first went to therapy, I thought that if I didn't remember it, I couldn't heal from it. That is entirely untrue.

You don't need to remember your childhood, your adolescence, or any event or period that felt stressful in order to heal. You don't need to dig up the messy details and relive them to move forward. You don't need to remember your childhood to connect with and soothe your childhood self. You can use what's available to you right now—your body, your emotions, and your inner experience— as a blueprint for what you could have been feeling then. We can use what's happening in the present moment as a way to heal from the past. All we have is what's here right now, and that's enough.

FAWNING SAFETY STRATEGY CHECKLIST

As we transition from childhood and adolescence to adulthood, the roles we played as safety strategies stay with us. We think: *This is what successfully protected me then, so this is what I'll keep doing.* Here are some of the most common ways in which a fawn response manifests in adult life. As you go through them, you may pause at each one and ask yourself: *When did I learn this was helpful or protective?*

- Constantly worrying what people think of you, if they like you, if they're mad at you
- Overextending yourself, not setting boundaries (and then feeling resentful)

- Avoiding conflict at all costs
- Constantly fearing getting in trouble or being seen as "bad"
- Constantly fearing that you *are* bad and you're just fooling everyone
- Constantly seeking external approval or validation
- Silencing your needs for the comfort and happiness of everyone else
- Feeling hypervigilant of people's emotions and moods
- Overexplaining yourself as an attempt to feel heard or understood
- Feeling like everything is your fault, and then overapologizing
- Being indecisive because you don't want to disappoint anyone or because you genuinely don't know what you like or prefer
- Not trusting yourself to make decisions
- Having trouble identifying your needs and speaking up about them
- Never feeling good enough; feeling unworthy of your accomplishments
- Constantly feeling like you're "performing" and trying to impress others and prove yourself to them
- Feeling like you're a chameleon in relationships

Fawning, at its core, is what we learn to do to avoid being abandoned or rejected and to maximize feelings of love and safety. The irony is that, in an unconscious attempt to avoid abandonment, we end up abandoning ourselves. For us to appease others to the degree that fawning requires, we have no choice but to fully disconnect from our own emotions, sensations, and needs. We're forced to withhold expressions of our sadness, fear, and anger to prevent conflict or negative reactions from our caregivers. But as we'll learn, these emotions, sensations, and needs don't just disappear—they go inward, toward ourselves, in the form of self-criticism and self-loathing.

When we're stuck in a constant fawn response, the behaviors just listed seep into all facets of our lives. The survival part of us thinks in black-and-white terms: *It's better for me to fawn every second, in every relationship, just in case.*

This isn't to say that we don't ever need to fawn. Fawning with your chaotic boss: sometimes actually necessary. Fawning with your partner, who is safe and understanding: not as necessary. When fawning is our default way of living, when we're fawning with our best friends, our partners, people who are safe and whom we don't need to fawn with—that's where the opportunity for healing is. And that's what this work is about: getting out of survival mode when we don't need to be in it. Think of chronic fawning as old software that needs an update. You're now on version 2.4, and the software is no longer compatible with your system.

FAMILIAR = SAFE

At this point, you're probably thinking, *Okay, cool, therapist lady. I get that fawning was protective for me then, so why am I stuck in it now?* If there's one thing from this chapter that I want you to remember, it's this:

What feels familiar to the body is going to feel safe.

What feels unfamiliar to the body is going to feel dangerous (even if it's not).

The primitive part of our brains—in other words, the part that is trying to keep us alive—tells us that safety lies in familiarity.[3] If people-pleasing and hypervigilance are familiar to the body because they are what have genuinely made us safe in our early environment and in society at large, that's what's going to feel safe to the body. We unconsciously gravitate toward situations that we've seen before because we know how to deal with them, even if they're toxic. We fulfill these fawning roles because that's what we know how to do. As we'll learn in the following chapters, when we're stuck in a trauma response, our bodies are frozen in that stressful event or period, and they will react from that place.

TRAUMA REENACTMENT

This unconscious attraction to what's familiar also explains why so many fawners unconsciously gravitate toward toxic work environments or relationships with emotionally unavailable or narcissistic people, because these environments and relationships mirror the chaos of childhood—they are what feels like home. To fawners, being the caretaker, being helpful, or being taken advantage of is a familiar dynamic. So when we meet someone who reminds us of our early relationships, we unconsciously think: *Oh yes, I've seen this before. I know how to do this. I know how to act with this person.*

We're often unconsciously drawn to relationships that remind us of past relationships (especially parental ones) that caused us pain, or that we didn't feel good enough in, so that we can unconsciously re-create those relationships and finally "fix" them and be enough for someone, thinking: *This time, I'll win. This time, I'll be enough for them, and it'll fix all the pain I felt from the original, hurtful relationship.* And we try harder and harder, we do more and more, in the hope that one day, the person we're with will change and we'll feel we are enough. But of course, we can't fix that person, because they were never emotionally capable of loving us in the way we deserve.

You win by grieving what you didn't get and moving forward to find what you truly deserve. We can break this unconscious pattern by bringing it into our conscious minds and asking ourselves: *What draws me to this person? Do I like them because they remind me of what I know, or because I genuinely feel safe and enjoy how I feel around them?*

On the flip side, anything that's unfamiliar to the body—like setting a boundary, saying no, speaking up, being with someone who's emotionally stable—is going to feel dangerous, because it's completely new. Clear, direct communication is going to feel like aggression if your baseline is people-pleasing. Hypervigilance is going to be your default state in adulthood if it's all you've known in your life thus far. Healthy, safe relationships are going to feel boring to your nervous system if chaos is all you've experienced. As we begin to heal this pattern together in the following chapters, we'll be slowly and subtly creating a new sense of what's familiar. We'll be creating new pathways in the brain, new ways of being.

A question to return to on this journey of healing is *Does this feel uncomfortable because it's unsafe, or is it just unfamiliar?*

Our early years have a deep, developmental impact on our self-beliefs, but that is not our destiny. Our brains are plastic—well, neuroplastic—which basically means that they have the ability to change and reorganize themselves. Michael Merzenich, a neuro-scientist and professor, performed research showing that the brain retains its ability to change, grow, and learn *throughout our entire lives.*[4] In other words, even if we've been stuck in a fawn response for decades, we're not screwed. Our brains were *made* to change.

Believe me when I say that most clients who come to me are stuck in a fawn response. So many people are. Let's start this work together by having you release the idea that something is wrong with you for being caught in this pattern of being, of overextend-ing, overapologizing, avoiding conflict, avoiding your needs. Instead of asking, "Why am I like this?" reframe it as "Of course I'm like this. It makes so much sense." You're a human being who learned to adapt in a way that made the most sense for you, in the environment that you were in, in a society and within systems that teach us to abandon ourselves for the comfort of other people. How brilliant of your past self for knowing what to do to keep the peace. How brilliant of your body for being able to read the room so aptly and create a safety system that genuinely worked. *Thank you, past self.* Now it's time for this part of you to get some much-needed rest.

REFLECTION QUESTIONS

1. In what ways did you fawn growing up? How did it protect you?
2. How does fawning pop up now in your everyday life, in ways that aren't as helpful?

Thank you, past self, for protecting me for so long. I am safe now.

CHAPTER

3

Permission to Heal

Acknowledging loss and processing grief

Meet Grief

My mom started to show symptoms of early-onset Alzheimer's when she was fifty-nine and I was nineteen. Cue the slow, painful grieving process of watching a parent disappear while they're still physically here on earth. Forgetting words in a conversation turned into forgetting to lock the front door, which, as the years passed, turned into forgetting the reality that we had shared. I also grieved the relationship that I wish we could've had, the closeness we weren't able to reach even in her healthy years.

My mom's mortality forced me to feel and accept the grief that was there all along. There's a rawness to grief; the core of my heart scooped out in the shape of the mom I'm yearning for. In grieving her, I grieved parts of my dad, too.

Grief isn't just about losing someone when they pass; it's also about what you didn't have. It's wanting to be nurtured but not having a parent who can nurture you. It's watching other families be with one another on holidays in a way you've only dreamed of. It's wanting to call your parent just to talk but knowing that they won't listen. It's a feeling of *I want to go home* when you're in your own family's house. It's knowing that you would be a family-oriented person if only you had a family to be that person with. It's letting go of that last sliver of hope that someone could change and be the person you need them to be. It's letting go of the hope for a childhood, a family, a parent relationship, a sibling relationship that you didn't have but deeply wanted. This, right here, is a necessary step in the fawner's healing process. We can't jump straight to acceptance and compassion without first acknowledging the ways in which it hurts, too.

When we're children, it's natural to put our caregivers on a pedestal and to fiercely protect the fantasy version we have of them. We naturally want them to be right and also to know everything, because if they don't, then who does? The world would seem too scary to a child if their parents weren't on a pedestal. As we get older and step into adulthood, we start to see that our parents are human and flawed, and they descend from that pedestal. Part of the grieving process is allowing that to happen. There can often be resistance to healing, because we still want to protect the vision of our parents that we hold so dear in our minds. But our healing isn't a betrayal of our parents.

I had a client who was told from a young age, directly and indirectly, that she was stupid. Her biggest insecurity as an adult was the fear of being seen as incompetent, as someone who couldn't figure it out on her own. This belief would follow her into adulthood disguised as impostor syndrome: *Who am I to be doing this? Why would anyone take me seriously?*

In our sessions, she realized that she was holding on to this belief that she was stupid because there was a younger part of her that still wanted her dad to be right. If he was right about her being stupid, then maybe he would be right about other things, and he could be someone she could rely on. Healing the limiting belief about her capability meant first accepting that her dad couldn't be the person she needed him to be, and then grieving the hope that he could be the parental figure she was protecting in her mind.

When I went to my first therapist, at twenty, so much of my initial resistance to listening to her was that I didn't want her to be right. I didn't want it to be true that my parents couldn't meet my emotional needs, because that would mean I'd need to confront the pain. That felt too foreign, and too scary, at the time.

Like any other aspect of your healing, grief isn't a checkbox item. It's a lingering weight that's always there, constantly changing form as you enter into and move out of different seasons of life. There's grief to be felt in realizing that your parents aren't capable of being the parents you need(ed) them to be. There's grief in realizing that your parents aren't your safe space or the people you call in an emergency. There's grief in realizing that you are your caregiver's emotional support system but they won't or can't be the same for you. There's grief in realizing that you shouldn't need to beg to have a close relationship with your parent. There's grief in becoming a parent yourself and not having a role model to look up to, relying on what you *didn't have* to create the vision of what you want for your own family. Acknowledging this grief is a crucial first step in your healing.

Meet Grief's Angsty Cousin

"Walk in like you own the place," my mom says to me. Her eyes are wide, almost urgent, as if she really needs me to listen. "That's what my mother used to tell me," she says.

You'd think I was going to interview for a job at Miranda

Priestly's office, but it was just my first day of middle school, which I guess is equally terrifying. We had just moved from Minnesota to Virginia, and I was entering arguably the most brutal school years with a gap between my front teeth so big my orthodontist said "a truck could drive through it" (direct quote), a plan to get braces, and no friends. As I step out the door to walk to the school bus, I look back at my mom once more, and she gives me a firm, encouraging nod, mouthing the words again in case I've already forgotten them: "Walk in like you own the place."

Later that day after school, my mom sits silent on the couch like a spectator, leaning back defeated as my dad spits out insults that'll later become my inner voice. I'm thirteen years old. With our recent move, I had hoped that we could leave Dad's darkness and depression behind along with the seemingly endless Minnesota winters. But the Virginia heat is only making things boil. His anger is worse now. *Maybe if we just moved somewhere else, the darkness wouldn't catch us.*

"What's wrong with you? I didn't do anything. I'm just reacting to *you*," he says.

My eyes dart to my mom as I wait for her to jump in and save me—do something, say something, anything. I'm angry at him, yes, but I'm angry at her in a different way. And maybe I'm angry at her because that's safer than being angry at him.

I'm angry that I'm defending her but she isn't doing the same for me. *I miss my mom*, I think to myself, even when she's sitting next to me. *Where did you go, and where have you been?*

And then I feel shame for being angry. *Does being angry make me a bad daughter?*

Out of exhaustion and the fact that there is nothing new to say, the battle comes to a close, and my dad trudges up the stairs, roaring a weekly declaration that he hates his life, and his words crawl into the deepest, most impressionable part of my being. My mom rolls her eyes in solidarity with me, and I retreat to the solace of my room, where I can let the anger alchemize into pain, allowing myself to cry now that I'm alone and can't be criticized for it.

As a teenager, keeping quiet started to feel like betraying myself, and my fear was blanketed by something more fiery. I had been taught up until that point that keeping quiet kept the peace, but then I realized it wasn't my peace I was keeping, and I was tired of it. My body was holding everyone's anger, and I didn't want to do that anymore. "Oh, you should be a lawyer," they'd say, but I just wanted to be heard.

For most of my life, I noticeably favored my dad over my mom. He was so unpredictable, yet I always gravitated toward him. It felt good to be chosen, and it felt safer to be under his wing than to be shoved aside. *I have two dads*, I would often think. *The one who's my best friend and the one who scares me.* The one who would snap at me without warning or reason and then would get me Skittles at the grocery store. I remember wishing that he was only mean, so then at least I could decide how I felt. His anger would creep out the most in the car and at home. I avoided bringing friends into either of these places. It felt too tiring, talking to my friends while holding my breath, keeping him in my peripheral vision, trying to control each environment so my friends wouldn't see what it was like when they were gone. I didn't want to perform, so I isolated myself instead. As an adolescent, I was the primary target for my dad's rage and criticism, and that was so confusing. *What is wrong with me? What about me causes so much unhappiness?* Because he couldn't manage his own emotions, I learned that maintaining his happiness was my job—and I always felt like I was about to get fired.

It's Okay to Be Angry

Morgan explains that her dad would be one person in public and an entirely different person in private. In public, he was warm, kind, and hilarious, and so proud of her, always bragging about her accomplishments to anyone who would listen. At home, he could flip like a switch, becoming highly reactive, critical, and verbally abusive. "It felt like he would just use my accomplishments to feed his own image," she explains. "The nice things he would say about me in front of other people, he never said to me. And then people would be like, 'I *love* your dad! He's the best!' but they had no idea of the person I knew, the side that I saw."

Anytime someone would compliment her dad, Morgan would feel viscerally angry, but she couldn't show it. When a child sees their parent exhibit two completely different sides, the child internalizes the belief that something is wrong with them because they get only the "bad" side and no one else does. A child thinks: *If other people see my parent as so warm and kind, why do I feel so hurt by them? It must be me; it must not be that bad. I must be bad to make them act so mean.*

Anger is part of the grieving process, but so many of us have been taught to believe that anger is bad, so we never fully grieve. If you only ever witnessed anger in extreme ways growing up, you learned: *Anger = unsafe. I must avoid anger at all costs, avoid conflict and disagreements. Anger is something to be feared.*

And when you felt anger growing up, how was it handled? For many of us, anger was punished or dismissed, or we were told not to feel it. So from that we learned: *Anger = bad, and when I feel anger, something is wrong with me for feeling it.* But anger, as we'll explore in chapter 5, is a natural, healthy human emotion that can be processed in a regulated way. How we react to the anger is our responsibility. But the anger is allowed to be there.

Acknowledging anger is one of the most important things for fawners to do. Anger is an emotion that has been swallowed again and again, for years and years. It's an emotion that is often followed by shame, which only suppresses the anger more. The irony is that when we can practice allowing anger to be there, there's way less opportunity for rage, because we're able to let the anger move through us. The healing begins when we can acknowledge our inner teenager who's starting to make sense of it all, or our inner self of whatever age comes to mind, and say to them, "You're allowed to be hurt and angry. Your anger makes sense and it deserves to be acknowledged. You're not bad for feeling angry."

Conflicting Truths

Multiple conflicting truths can exist at the same time. You can be grateful for what your parents could give you emotionally *and* feel grief for what they couldn't. You can have empathy for what your parents have gone through themselves, for the trauma they must have survived, *and* feel angry that you experienced what you did. You can acknowledge that your parents did their best with the awareness and resources they had at the time *and* acknowledge that their best still *really* hurt you.

No one emerges from childhood unscathed, and there's no such thing as a "perfect" parent. I like to think that a parent's weakness becomes the child's strength, and that's how we evolve as a collective. I trust that my mom was as nurturing to me as she could have been to herself, and as nurturing as her mom was to her, and that my dad, in some ways, must have done a better job than his dad. Although these thoughts don't negate the pain and neglect that I endured, it feels freeing to remind myself that my parents' pain wasn't my fault and I didn't do anything to deserve it. My parents often talked about how their parents were very controlling, micromanaging what they should do for work and with their lives and strictly defining what was "good" and "right." With my brothers and me, they broke that pattern in the way they knew how, letting us choose our own career paths without much pressure or input—except when I was eleven and left the movie theater with my dad after watching *Dream Girls*, remnants of blue-and-red slushy melting in my cup, and declared that I wanted to be an actress. (My parents said, "No, you can't do that or you'll become a drug addict and die.") But apart from being an actress, I really thought I could do anything. They allowed me to explore what I was interested in, and they never put excessive pressure on me, in part because I had the pressure department covered all by myself.

Having a parent who is emotionally immature, unpredictable, highly self-focused, or hypercritical, a child often learns that being a high achiever is how to stay under that parent's wing and maintain the golden status bestowed by that parent. When love is conditional, achieving is one of the few things a child can control to increase their odds of receiving attention and approval. My whole life, I unconsciously put so much pressure on myself to achieve so that I could keep my parents' unhappiness at bay and bask in the warmth of my dad's approval. It felt special to be seen as special.

Sometimes they went too far with the freedom they granted me. What might have seemed like freedom to them sometimes felt like emotional neglect to me. They weren't just hands-off with my career path. They loved me, I knew that, but did they know me?

When I was younger, this gap was more felt than noticed. As I entered my twenties and my mom was no longer around to be the bridge for my communication with my dad ("Do you want to talk to Dad? Let me pass the phone over"), our relationship was stripped down to its barest form and I was able to see it more clearly. I realized that I was always the one to call and check in, and that my dad reached out only when he needed something from me (advice, a confidence boost, money). I'd beg him to be interested in my life, to be part of it, and I didn't know if it was supposed to be that hard to have a close-ish relationship with your parent. *At least he doesn't yell at me much these days*, I'd bargain with myself.

In the spirit of fawning, I thought that if I just kept trying harder, maybe something would change. I thought that if I could get closer to perfection, maybe I'd have the relationship with my dad that I wanted.

I can see now that my parents' behaviors weren't a reflection of my deservingness or an indicator that I wasn't doing enough to earn parental love. My parents healed the generational patterns that they were capable of healing, and I'm healing the ones that they couldn't.

You Could Be Waiting Forever

"I just want him to see how much he hurt me," Alex explains. "Then I can move on."

For years, Alex has been waiting for an apology from her dad, or at least an acknowledgment of the pain and loneliness she endured because of his emotional neglect.

"That makes so much sense. But the truth is that an apology may never happen. Does that mean you can't ever heal?" I ask.

In any sort of conflict, whether it's a parental wound or a nasty breakup, we often wait for an external cue (an apology, an acknowledgment, tears with snot) to begin our healing. What I like to remind clients, and myself, is that people can meet us only as far as they've met themselves.

If our parents were capable of causing that much pain, a lot of healing would have to happen for them to gain enough awareness to take accountability for that pain. Waiting for an external cue to allow us to move forward puts our healing in the other person's hands and often comes from a fantasy that that person will change. But what if they don't? Through this fantasy of the other person apologizing or changing, the mind is seeking false control over pain. The mind thinks: *Maybe once I hear "I'm sorry," it won't hurt so bad.*

We can start healing when we stop trying to get our pain validated by the people who caused us harm. So often we look for external validation from those who aren't emotionally capable of seeing the pain they caused and may never be capable of doing that in this lifetime. Repeating yourself or trying to prove yourself to someone who's emotionally immature will not work and will keep you stuck in the cycle of pain, anger, and disempowerment. You can begin to move forward when you can accept this reality—and give the younger version of you the validation you've been craving: *I believe you. What you went through was really hard, and it wasn't your fault. You didn't deserve that. It's no longer your job to try to make them understand.*

Moving forward isn't synonymous with "getting over it" or shoving aside your emotions.

It means allowing yourself to see and hold the pain in ways that you wish the other person could. It means moving forward *while* feeling the loss. It's not getting over the loss so that you can move forward; it's moving forward *with* the feeling of loss, soothing it whenever it arises.

In my personal experience and in witnessing clients' healing from wounded parental relationships, a child wants a healthy, functional relationship with their parent and will look past many things in order to have it. I've seen many adult children forgive their parents for endless past trauma so that they can have some sort of relationship with them. Adult children can understand that their parents endured their own traumatic experiences and have empathy for them. The biggest pain point that prevents present closeness is the parent still behaving the same way, when the parent isn't capable of acknowledging the past and working on themself in the present. When parents know better and are still behaving harmfully, it feels like they are making an active choice to do so, and that causes more grief and pain.

With a parent, or with anyone who is staying the same while you're growing, it hurts. Perhaps the work, then, is not about trying to change them or the relationship; maybe it's about changing your relationship *to* the relationship. Maybe externally, in the relationship itself, there won't be any noticeable changes. Maybe the work is an internal shift, releasing expectations that the relationship can or will look any different than it does, and processing the pain that goes with that realization.

It's not that grief disappears but that it starts to feel normal, and life forms around it—but we must first acknowledge it.

Emotional Loneliness

Growing up with emotionally neglectful or immature parental figures can be confusing, because you might have all your physical needs met and still feel empty. Having caregivers who don't provide a safe emotional connection can lead to deep emotional loneliness in childhood and adulthood, feeling like you need to hide who you are because it was once risky to fully show yourself or, when you do get close to someone, feeling like there's still something missing. To a kid, emotional loneliness just feels . . . normal. It's an ever-looming separateness, a barrier, a disconnection, even when you're in the same room as your family. It's a feeling of emptiness, a loneliness, that lives deep in your gut. You may feel like you're constantly chasing a feeling of home, of nostalgia for something you've been craving your whole life.

Even as a child gets older, even if they're independent in other ways, they crave the emotional presence of a parent. I find that the wounds of emotional neglect get amplified in early adulthood, when people no longer have the convenience of living under the same roof as their parents. When there's no longer built-in small talk over dinner or chatter about Halloween costumes, there's a gap in connection that has to be filled. When you're living in different places, someone has to be the one to call first. Someone has to be the one to show interest in the other person's now physically separate life. For those who have endured emotional neglect, there's often a harsh realization that they are going to be the one to carry the relationship, and that maybe that distance was there all along. Emotional loneliness can be felt even if someone talks to their parent every day. It's not just about the act of physically speaking; it's the emotional distance within the relationship, the lack of depth, not feeling known by the parent.

I have this memory from when I was in middle school, in gym class outdoors, walking with my close friend at a pace slow enough for us to debrief last night's episode of *American Idol* but quick enough to keep our gym teacher from noticing that we aren't running. The late-September Virginia sun is strong against the back of my neck, and there's dust from the gravel track loop floating in the air, coating my hands and arms in a thin layer. I don't remember what my friend and I were talking about exactly; I just remember having a sudden, distinct panic. It was not so much granular thought as an existential feeling: *Does my close friend feel close to me? Or is her version of closeness something even closer, something I can't possibly feel?*

This idea of closeness always confused me. *Am I doing relationships right? Should I feel closer to people than this?* Even now, it's so hard to put that feeling into words. I remember saying to this same friend, "Do you ever wonder what the point is of getting close to someone if they're just gonna have to leave?" I tried to frame it as a joke, but I genuinely wanted to know if she thought about this, too.

As I entered my late teens, this question continued to nag at me when I started to get close to someone. Over time I began to wonder if the closeness I was searching for and constantly feared I was lacking was rooted in something much deeper, from when I was much younger. *Is the emotional closeness I always fear I'm missing a reflection of the closeness I wasn't able to feel with my parents?* Emotional loneliness stemming from childhood is a vague, looming experience. It's a cloud, a feeling that something is wrong but you just can't figure out what.

Often this loneliness is masked by hyperindependence, a deep-rooted belief that you need to handle everything on your own, that it's unsafe to ask for help or rely on others, because you had to be your own parent when you were so young. I cultivated the skills of taking care of myself from an early age—heating up my own soup when I was sick, grocery shopping and cooking my own meals as soon as I got my driver's license, so that I could mother myself. I learned early on that I *could* fully rely on myself, but those skills don't soothe the loneliness beneath.

When a client says, "I don't need anyone; I can handle everything on my own," that often translates in my therapist-brain to *When I did need someone, no one was there, so I've learned that it's safer to keep people at a distance than to risk letting people in and being let down (again).* Despite fawning being a "nice" threat response that can flood us with short-term validation and bursts of affirmation, it ultimately maintains the distance that's so familiar to us. Fawning keeps us from being vulnerable, honest. It lets people in on the surface but emotionally keeps people at a distance. Fawning pushes away authentic connection for the sake of short-term harmony. How close we can get to other people is a direct reflection of how close we are to ourselves.

Feeling Behind, Moving Forward

"I feel like I'm chronically behind in life, like there was some new-student orientation on the first day of adulthood that I must have missed, some guidebook on how to do life that I must not be aware of," says Clara. Another common experience for fawners—or for anyone who was in survival mode growing up—is feeling like they're constantly "behind" in life.

On top of living in a society that is constantly telling us we're not doing enough, that we should accomplish more and weigh less, this feeling of being behind is common for people who grew up in a chaotic environment. While you were focused on surviving, mediating relationships, and maximizing moods, others your age who grew up in more emotionally stable environments had the time to develop, explore, learn, grow, and get to know themselves. All the years you've spent fawning weren't time wasted. We can acknowledge the grief for the years that we've fawned without adding a layer of self-loathing. Remember, fawning has been an unconscious survival response. All we can do is thank this protective part of ourselves for taking care of us for so long and cultivate the skills and awareness to move forward with a deeper understanding of it. *Thank you, protective part. It's time for you to rest now. You don't need to work so hard anymore.*

Deep wounds have many layers, and not being "over it" doesn't mean you haven't healed—perhaps you now feel safe enough in your body to access a deeper, raw layer that's been waiting to be seen. Healing from this loss starts with acknowledging it. Putting language to it, even simply saying "This is grief" when it arises, helps. Grief comes in waves, not steps.

When I went home for Christmas at age twenty-one, I grieved my mom each time she asked me the same question three times in one conversation and swallowed my fear so as not to provoke hers. When I was twenty-seven, I grieved my mom as I walked down the aisle on my wedding day without her there, because she had moved into a full-time memory care facility a year earlier. As I write this now, she's at the tail end of her life, and I grieve my mom as I see my friends getting closer to their moms, as their moms go from being their moms to also being their friends. I grieve my mom who is dying, and I grieve the close relationship I didn't have with her when she was living. And while I grieve her, I also grieve the dad who's still here but doesn't always feel like he is. Grief doesn't go away—it's part of my body's topography, like rivers and creeks carved into me—but it morphs and changes and moves from the foreground to the background, then to the foreground again. Time keeps passing, and life keeps going—as do we.

Healing this loss means seeing your parents objectively, realizing that their pain and emotional distance were never your fault and their patterns aren't proof that something is wrong with you. No child can be "good enough" to earn a functional childhood when their parents are in so much pain of their own and are stuck in their own unprocessed trauma. The causes and conditions that have led us here aren't our fault, but our healing is our responsibility. And by holding this book in your hands and beginning the journey of creating a relationship with your inner experience, you're already doing it.

REFLECTION QUESTIONS

1. Is there something that you're grieving? Notice if any resistance comes up as you acknowledge it—that's okay.

2. Is there something you feel angry about? (You're allowed to feel angry.)

3. As you reflect on your past, are conflicting emotions coming up for you?

I am allowed to acknowledge the loss that I feel. I can give myself the validation that others can't.

CHAPTER

You Are Not Your Thoughts

Introducing NICER

Noticing the Inner Voice

"Okay, but how do I *stop* the anxious thoughts?" Mia asks. We've just finished a mindfulness exercise in which she spent five minutes simply observing her inner dialogue. I ask how it felt for her, what she noticed, and she describes some of the places that her mind dragged her to: her grocery list, how maybe she doesn't deserve the raise she wants to ask for, a text she forgot to reply to, how she overshared at her office holiday party last week (that came up many times), and feeling annoyed at herself for not being able to sit still for five minutes.

Many clients come to therapy with an urgency to "fix" themselves and get rid of the loud, anxious inner voice. (For the record, I was also that client.) They're often surprised, and maybe even skeptical, when I tell them that the goal of this work isn't to silence the anxious voice—trying to silence it only makes it louder—but to start becoming aware of it, attaching to it less, and soothing it. The most important aspect of your healing is your own awareness. It's realizing that you aren't the voice inside your mind; you're the one who notices it.

That voice talks all day long, commenting on everything, fixating on the past, worrying about the future. The human mind thinks—that's what it does. It's actually kind of shocking when you start to notice how much the mind talks. Does it not have anything better to do?

Take a moment to pause and notice the thoughts that are popping into your head. I invite you to put the book down and just observe what thoughts are visiting, even just for ten seconds.

Did you hear the chatter?

Thoughts Aren't the Ultimate Truth

Thoughts are like little clouds passing through your mind. As you begin to notice your inner chatter, you'll probably see how quick we can be to believe the fearful thoughts yet shoo away the hopeful, optimistic ones. The fact that it's a thought doesn't mean it's the truth. And even still, something can be true without being *the* truth. Self-deprecating, anxiety-driven thoughts can feel so much more believable (*I'm unlovable and I'm going to be alone forever*) than thoughts that could invite possibility (*I'm worthy of being loved exactly as I am, including my messy parts*) because our brains are hardwired to worry. This voice in our heads is often scared and is bringing past experiences into the present moment. We can acknowledge the voice while knowing that it isn't always *right*. The experience of what we're feeling is real, but the thoughts surrounding those feelings aren't always true.

Anxious Thoughts and the Illusion of Control

A key idea in Buddhism is that worrying about or fixating on a scenario gives us a false sense of control. Fawners often are waiting for the worst-case scenario to occur and have trouble believing it when good things happen, because they have always needed to be on guard.

When we are adults, this protective mechanism manifests as overthinking: *Maybe if I think about this worst-case scenario thirty-seven times, I'll be prepared when (if) it happens. If I play out every possible angle of the imaginary conversation, maybe I'll know exactly what to say or do if the conversation happens, and I'll feel in control of the uncomfortable emotions that I'll inevitably feel.* We repeatedly play out the worst thing that could happen to control how we'll *feel* if it does. If the worst-case scenario brings up a lot of fear, or anger, or guilt, we'll imagine that scenario again and again so that we can figure out what to do with the discomfort of those emotions.

Even though we really *don't* have control over the random events that will come our way or how a conversation is going to go, that's a hard pill to swallow for the mind, which finds safety in certainty. The practice is to recognize the limits of our control. Research has actually found that while we may believe thinking about the worst-case scenario will help us emotionally prepare for it, such thinking often does not alleviate our distress when the anticipated event actually occurs. Instead, it increases anxiety and stress during the anticipation phase without significantly reducing the emotional impact of the event itself.[1] Fixating on the worst-case scenario repeatedly doesn't make that scenario any easier if it even happens; it just adds more suffering. Our brains and bodies don't know the difference between an imagined experience and an actual experience. Physiologically, they feel the same. So when we torture ourselves with the worst possibility and it actually does happen, we're living it twice—once in our heads, and then again in reality.

People-pleasing is an unconscious way of trying to feel a false sense of control (with emphasis on "unconscious"—remember that fawning is an adaptive survival mechanism). It's when we can be *aware* that we're fawning that we can begin to break out of the pattern. People-pleasing makes us feel safe by allowing us to feel in control of the narrative, of people's perceptions—all to avoid our own discomfort, to avoid our own emotions, which feel scary to sit with.

A client once said to me, "What would I even think about if I weren't anxious? Like, where would my focus be?" Underneath the need to control is discomfort. By fixating, we put off looking at and feeling the uncomfortable emotions that linger beneath the surface. On the other side of that discomfort is freedom. It's time for you to start trusting your future self to carry you through difficult situations—your future self has always gotten you through before.

The Subconscious Storyteller: Understanding Your Inner Critic

Recurrent thoughts are rooted in the subconscious. Think of this inner voice as a tape recorder storing everything we've witnessed and heard from our siblings, bullies, friends, society, the media, and especially our parents. This background noise often comes from the internalized voices of the people who raised us, as the recycled words of our parents speaking out of dysregulation. From the time we are at an early age, these voices become the subconscious beliefs we hold about ourselves.[2] We see the world, our relationships, and ourselves through our subconscious beliefs, and our brains look for information to affirm these beliefs, to prove them to be true.[3] So if your conditioned belief is *When people are in a bad mood, it's my fault* or *No one likes me,* your brain will surely find ways to prove these beliefs are true, like scanning people's faces to see if they thought your joke was funny (and overanalyzing their reactions).

Meet the harsh inner critic many of us developed in childhood as a stand-in for the support we needed.

In Internal Family Systems therapy, we think of the self as being made up of many "parts" that serve important, protective functions. These parts are like little beings who live within you, trying their best to keep you safe and to keep the "system" within you running smoothly.[4] They just want safety, and when you're stuck in a fawn response, there's a scared part of you that you're not conscious of that thinks it needs to work hard to make sure no one's upset, everyone likes you, and no conflict is about to erupt, because those thoughts were once extremely necessary and effective. This part was once constantly on duty, but it hasn't gotten the memo that it doesn't need to be working overtime anymore.

I like to visualize this scared part as a younger version of myself, tugging at my hand, trying to get my attention. If you don't connect with the term "inner child" or "inner teenager," it may feel easier to think of it as just *you*. After all, this younger version of you lived in the same body that you live in now.

If picturing your younger self is still hard to do, it may be helpful to think of this voice as an animal or a character of some sort. For whatever reason, the image that comes to mind for me is Totoro from the film *My Neighbor Totoro*, who is an adorable woodland creature with tall ears, wide eyes, and a squishy belly. When you can picture this scared voice coming from a being separate from you, whether it's a younger version of you or a fictional character, it will be easier to remember that those thoughts are not you, that you are the one listening.

In a way, the harsh inner critic became someone who had your back, a voice of guidance to protect you, to parent you, or to help you get ahead of the criticism you might've received from others. If you're critical of yourself first, you can be "perfect," someone whom no one will find fault with. Think of this critic as your inner adviser, a concerned friend working tirelessly to keep you safe. Your inner critic put tons of pressure on you and learned what sorts of things attracted criticism or sparked conflict, and it learned what to say to get you to prevent those things from happening. The inner critic is trying to protect you, but that doesn't mean you always need protecting. So many fawners have such harsh inner critics because there once wasn't space for their uncomfortable emotions like anger, sadness, and fear. Those emotions couldn't be expressed and they had to go somewhere, so they went inward, toward the self, manifesting as harsh self-criticism.

Challenging Our Perception

Compliments can provoke anxiety when we're stuck in a fawn response with low self-esteem because they challenge our perception of what's true and familiar.

For Ari, fawning and low self-image manifest as deflecting compliments with self-deprecating humor and constantly diminishing herself. In her free time, Ari works tirelessly on her graphic design business with the hope of eventually quitting her day job. But when she's out with a friend, getting to know some new faces, her friend compliments Ari's work and nudges her to share more about it with everyone, and Ari makes fun of herself: "Oh, it's stupid. Just a silly little side thing I do."

So much of fawning is making other people feel comfortable, or even superior, so that we can feel safe. A compliment feels like a threat to the body: *Deflect so they know you're humble and good! Don't feel threatened by me; I'm just a nobody.* This is the same reason fawning can make you feel unworthy of your accomplishments. The inner critic (which is trying to protect you) tells you that no accomplishment is enough because it's stuck in a time when you had to constantly impress in order to achieve a sense of safety. The fawn response is about finding safety by doing more: if you reached the point where you felt "good enough," that protective part would feel scared because it would mean you could stop trying so hard.

Because fawners often struggle with low self-esteem, it can feel like no accomplishment is impressive. If you were able to achieve it, then it must not be that important or have been that hard, leading you to constantly undervalue your milestones. Nothing is enough for the inner critic who's trying so hard to find safety through perfection. Achievements may bring a sense of relief instead of joy, because those achievements were merely an obligation, another milestone you had to complete to continue to prove yourself. Receiving compliments challenges Ari's core belief of her unworthiness (*I'm not good enough*), so she pushes them away.

She wants to reject herself before others can reject her. She doesn't think she's enough, so it feels absolutely unbelievable to her when someone else thinks she is. At the same time, she feels frustrated by her inability to accept praise, because she desperately wants to be taken seriously.

Our work together started with noticing what these beliefs were and where they came from, and then it continued with processing the pain beneath them. As Ari started to become aware of the voice of her storyteller and where these ideas originated (her parents), she was slowly able to give the voice less power, talk to herself in a new way, and rewrite the story herself.

Releasing the Fear of Our Thoughts

I once worked with Emma, who felt deep shame for having critical thoughts about other people. She'd notice a critical thought pop up about her partner and then would immediately feel shame for having had the thought and beat herself up. Emma would convince herself she was a horrible person and a horrible partner, and she'd even feel the need to confess her thoughts to her partner, although the thoughts were involuntary. *Am I a bad person?* she'd ask herself.

By working on simply noticing the thoughts and allowing them to be there, over time Emma was able to soften her relationship to those thoughts. She realized that the critical thoughts she was having were things she was telling herself. In a way, she was judging other people through the judgments she had about herself.

I see this fear fed by language like "Thoughts create reality" and "Every cell of your body is listening to your thoughts." *Am I manifesting bad things in my life if I'm having a fearful thought?* As a result, we can easily become tyrants over our thoughts, shoving thoughts away as soon as they enter for fear that they'll come true.

While our thoughts certainly have enormous power, perhaps it's more accurate to say that our *focus* creates our reality. What we pour our *attention* into is what shapes our lives. So many of our thoughts are involuntary, and when we relate to them with fear and rigidity, we only make them louder. Our thoughts are not actions. What we *do* with our thoughts and with our emotions—*that's* our responsibility and *that's* what's in our control.

But the mind oftentimes conjures weird and random thoughts, and it can bombard us. So many of us are constantly overthinking—and feeling shame for our thoughts. The mind thinks, overthinks, ruminates—that's what it does. Nothing is "wrong" with you for having critical or challenging thoughts, and you are not "bad" for having them.

We tend to pick fights with our inner voices as a way to feel in control of them. We try to silence these voices and shut them up by resisting them (*I want this to go away! How do I make it stop?*), but this only adds more mental tension. The funny thing is, these efforts just become the same voice fighting with itself. We unconsciously think that if we are fighting our inner voices, they'll stop. But that never works.

Soothing the Scared Voice

If that scared part of you, that harsh inner voice, is a younger version of yourself, then relating to that part of yourself with shame and hatred means that you're replicating the cycle that was modeled for you. If you're screaming at the scared part of yourself, wishing it would go away, of course it's still scared. It's being treated as it has been all along. By wanting it to go away, you're still telling that scared part that something is inherently wrong with it. The scared part isn't something to get rid of; it's a part of you that's *starving for love and acceptance*. If you don't soothe that inner voice, the need to soothe and protect it will never go away. If you had a beloved pet that was scared, you wouldn't soothe it by saying, "What's *wrong* with you? You shouldn't be scared. Get over it." No, of course not.

You'd gently approach your pet, offer your hand, and say, "What's wrong? What do you need? You're okay." How is this scared part of yourself, the part that chronically fawns, any different?

Talk to this part of yourself the way you'd talk to a toddler. The next time you accidentally break a glass and your inner voice starts berating you, pause and shift the dialogue: *Oops, that's okay. Mistakes happen. You don't need to be perfect.* The next time this younger part feels scared, you might just say to yourself, *That's okay. You're safe.* This might feel ridiculous at first, but perhaps that just goes to show how unfamiliar self-compassion has been to you.

If you find it challenging to relate to your scared inner voice with compassion, it can be helpful to create some sort of Compassionate Other, a framework used in Compassion-Focused Therapy, or CFT. A Compassionate Other is a being that is compassionate, wise, calm, and grounded and can talk to and relate to the scared parts of you on your behalf. This Compassionate Other can be the most evolved version of you, or it can be someone in your life who feels safe and secure to you, or it can be a fictional character from a movie or a book or is completely made up but whom you would find comforting to have around. Are they younger or older than you? What are they wearing? What does their voice sound like? What does their face look like? This person or being will never criticize you or blame you but will always remain understanding, calm, and nurturing.

Remember, the scared part of you serves a protective function—we all *need* this part, just not all the time. You're watching the mind do its little dance. You can relate to this scared part, frozen in time, in the way that you wished your parents had related to you when you were growing up. You can give it the love, acceptance, and care that it's been waiting for. This is where the healing is. You could soothe this voice with statements like these:

- I know that you're scared right now. It's okay, I'm here.
- You're safe now. I'm the parent and I'll take care of you.
- I see that you're overthinking again. That's okay. Thank you for trying to protect me.
- You're allowed to be here. I'm not trying to get rid of you, but you don't need to work so hard.

The Myth About Mindfulness

"I keep having anxious thoughts while I meditate. What am I doing wrong?" one of my classmates asks during my first meditation training.

I'm twenty-two, living in New York, one of seventeen students sitting cross-legged on cushions in a semicircle. Our teacher pauses, absorbing the question, and my classmates and I nod, eagerly awaiting a single, succinct answer that'll—*poof*—dissolve our overthinking.

"You're doing it right, then. You're seeing what's there," the teacher says.

Huh?

It felt like the first time I didn't need to try so hard to be "successful" at something. So much of fawning is learning that you need to do more and more and more in order to be loved and to feel safe. It felt like such a relief—and equally confusing—that the practice was simply allowing my inner experience to be okay.

When I first started meditating, I would get so pissed at myself. I'd plop down on my cushion each morning, close my eyes, release a sharp exhale, and wait for calm to wash over me. *If I'm doing this "right," shouldn't I be calm the whole time?* I thought the presence of anxiety or racing thoughts was proof that I was somehow doing it wrong. Perhaps this was simply reflecting how I thought my emotions were "wrong" off the cushion, out in the world. I fought everything I was thinking and feeling.

Ironically, this pressure to feel calm in my practice was what was causing so much of my suffering. My relationship to mindfulness practices shifted when I realized that they were not about trying to feel calm but instead about allowing whatever was arising to be there, without trying to change it, control it, or judge it. I recently had the privilege of attending one of Buddhist teacher Sylvia Boorstein's silent retreats. She described how mindfulness allowed her to feel "the full emotional palette." I used to think that being mindful meant that I had to be a boring being without personality, whereas really, mindfulness leads us to being deeply and authentically connected to ourselves, to our internal world, and to the world around us.

Being present doesn't mean feeling good all the time. I repeat: Being present doesn't always equal feeling good.

It's easy for perfectionism to creep into your mindfulness practice, leading you to treat it like another class that you need to excel in. Of course. The mind doesn't know the difference between mindfulness and any other facet of your life. There's no such thing as doing mindfulness "wrong," because it's simply a practice of paying attention, of noticing what's happening right now. When you do get caught up in a spiral of judging yourself for thinking, don't judge yourself for judging yourself. Just notice that voice, too.

The inner voice will always find something to be dissatisfied with, something to comment on and critique, something that you need to be working on in order to be as close to "perfect" as you can (and the closer you get, the farther ahead the finish line in front of you just keeps getting pushed).

People often think that mindfulness is escapism, a way to leave reality. But mindfulness is really providing us with the ability to *be with* reality. Mindfulness trains us to deal with what life throws at us with a sense of inner stability instead of turning away from it. It's not about getting rid of stressors or falsely believing that there's a magical land in the clouds of our mind where stress doesn't exist. Rather, we're altering how we relate to the stress so that we don't make things harder than they need to be. Practicing mindfulness doesn't change what's happening—it changes our capacity to be with what is.

The Power of Labeling

Labeling is one of my favorite mindfulness practices. There's a relief that comes from taking the chaos and vastness of our thoughts, the messiness of our emotions, and saying, "This is just what's happening." When we find ourselves overthinking, we don't necessarily need to dig into the thoughts themselves and pick them apart. We can instead notice, *I am overthinking*, focusing more on the shape of the thoughts, the rhythm of them, than on the thoughts themselves. The mind wants to get pulled into the details of the thoughts in an attempt to figure them out. Put that urge down for a second and practice simply noticing that you were thinking.

Charlie was a history teacher who had had a lifelong dream of writing novels. On the weekends Charlie would hibernate with his computer and write, getting lost in the stories of the worlds he created. He had three finished novels, which were sitting idly in his documents folder. I watched as his face lit up when he was telling me about the stories he'd written, and then something shifted. The twinkle left his eyes and his face dropped and became clouded with fear as he got lost in thought.

"Where did you just go?" I asked.

"I don't know. I feel so stupid. I don't know why I thought this could work or why I ever thought I could actually be a writer. What makes me think I could ever do that?" he whispered.

"It sounds like the self-doubt is really strong right now," I said.

He lifted his head slowly to look at me. "Self-doubt? I guess that's what this is. It sounds so . . . normal when you say it like that."

By labeling the experience as self-doubt, Charlie was able to remember that *these were just thoughts,* not the ultimate truth. By labeling it as a common human experience that many people, including other creatives, feel, he was able to feel less isolated.

Another key idea in Buddhism is that we tend to cling or attach to what feels pleasant (like the pleasure of eating chocolate), have an aversion to what feels unpleasant (like the discomfort of setting a boundary), and feel nothing toward or even detached from things that feel neutral (like breathing—it's kind of just there). This makes sense. We like what feels good (and comfortable) and we don't like what feels uncomfortable (largely because it's simply unfamiliar). We can practice labeling our inner experiences this way as well.

In Buddhism, this is called Vedanā, or feeling tones, which means labeling our inner experiences as pleasant, unpleasant, or neutral. This simple technique allows us to acknowledge our thoughts without identifying with them or acting on them.

Be Nicer to Yourself

NICER (Notice, Invite, Curiosity, Embrace, and Return) is a tool to keep in your pocket to help you in moments of anxious panic. Fawning conditions the mind to ruminate and fixate. The practice of NICER cultivates an awareness that's stronger than our thoughts.

It's been a long week at work. Every therapy slot has been filled, my energy has been depleted, and I'm relieved to see "Friday, 5:32 p.m." on the top right corner of my computer screen. My thoughts are drifting to running a hot bath when I see a text and hear a *ding* right next to the time: "I know it's last minute but do you wanna go to this concert with me tonight?? Could be fun!" my friend has texted, sending the link to the tickets.

My immediate, visceral reaction is *Oh noooo. I'm so tired.* Sign number one of what my body needs. I respond quickly and easily, thanking her for the invite but saying that I'm exhausted and want to go to bed early tonight, and she replies, "Totally understand! See you Sunday ☺." (We have an intricate plan to get veggie banh mi sandwiches and then go to the de Young Museum in San Francisco. The perfect Sunday.)

A few minutes pass, and then I suddenly feel nauseated by guilt. The thoughts rush in: *Am I a bad friend? Maybe I should have just pushed through and said yes. But my immediate reaction was ugh . . . But maybe a good friend would suck it up and go anyway. But I'm seeing her on Sunday; it's fine. What if she doesn't text me in the future about this kind of stuff? What if she thinks I'm a "no" girl? What if she thinks I don't like hanging out with her?* My mind fights with itself.

I reach for my phone and begin to type: "Actually, maybe I can go"—and then I stop. Pause. *Why was I so confident about my deci-*

sion two minutes ago, and now I'm suddenly switching? Do I actually want to go, or do I just not want to sit with the discomfort of feeling guilty about being honest about what I need?

I put my phone down, far enough away that I can't reach it, and I take a seat.

I first **notice (N)** what's happening internally. *I'm noticing that I'm overthinking, and I'm noticing that I'm feeling guilt and anxiety.* I then **invite (I)** this experience to be here. I allow it to exist without immediately trying to fix it or change it. I silently say to myself, *This is allowed to be here. This is okay.* I notice a little discomfort in allowing the experience to stay, and that's just noticed, too. I then bring in some **curiosity (C)**, as if I'm gathering field notes on my mind and body. What part of me has been activated? What is it that I'm feeling? Can I put a label on this experience? *Yes, this is guilt. Mixed with some anxiety. That's what this is. I'm feeling like a bad friend.* Am I noticing bodily sensations that go with these feelings? *Mmmm, tightness in the chest, and my throat feels clenched.* I then **embrace (E)** this part of me as if I were wrapping it in a blanket. *I see you, protective part. Thank you for trying to help me. It's okay that this feeling is here. I'm safe. This is okay.* Then I **return (R)** to what's real and true right now: the sensation of my breath, any sounds in the room, the feeling of my feet on the ground. By returning to tangible things that are real and true right now, in *this* moment, I'm pulling my focus back into the present.

I open my eyes, look at the clock, and see that only three minutes have passed, yet I feel so different than I did before. It's not that the anxiety is gone, or the tightness is gone, but I'm no longer consumed by it. By allowing myself to pause, I was able to keep myself from reacting from a dysregulated place and return to the present.

After nearly a decade of daily meditation (though I have so much more to learn) and years of using NICER in my everyday life, the anxiety hasn't magically disappeared for me, but it doesn't have as much power as it used to.

I still have lots of anxious thoughts; I just don't believe them as much anymore.

I still overthink and ruminate and fixate from time to time, but I'm able to return to a place of groundedness much more quickly, and with more self-forgiveness. The noise is still there, but most of the time it's playing in the background, not the foreground. The chaos is still happening; I just don't view it as *me* anymore.

When I look back on how stuck in the anxiety I felt ten years ago, the difference is astounding. Now I'm not going into my mindfulness practice with the expectation that it's supposed to eliminate my very human inner experience or the pressure for it to do so. I'm going into it saying: *Let's just see what's happening here and now.*

Now that you've seen NICER in practice, let's look at how you can use it in your everyday life when you're caught up in overthinking.

NOTICE. Notice that your mind started anxiously spiraling. Notice that you got lost in an imaginary conversation. Notice that you just took a one-way trip to a worst-case scenario. That's it, just notice that your mind went there. No need to add an extra layer of self-judgment for having the thought. Just notice that your mind was thinking.

INVITE. Invite this inner experience to stay just for a second like an old friend; allow it to exist. This isn't to say that you're clinging to the thought; rather, you're just not resisting it or shoving it away. *It's okay that this is here. Nothing is wrong with me for thinking or feeling this. This is just what's happening now, and it's impermanent.* Or even more simply, you can say to yourself, *Just this.*

CURIOSITY. Allow curiosity in. Be the observer of your own body and mind. Not in an overthinking, overintellectualizing way but in a grounded, clear manner. *Is this thought true? What emotion is this? What bodily sensations am I experiencing right now? Are these sensations pleasant, unpleasant, or neutral?*

EMBRACE. Embrace this protective part of you, this inner voice, with warmth and understanding. The mind's tendency is to make us judge ourselves for having an anxious thought (*Why am I like this? When will this go away?*). We're working on relating to our inner experience with a bit more compassion. *Thank you for trying to protect me. It's okay that you're feeling this. It makes sense. You're safe.*

RETURN. Return to something that's real and true right now. This could be the steady rise and fall of your belly as you breathe in and out, a siren you hear in the distance, or a sensation in your body. By gently shifting your focus to what's happening now, you're training your mind to return to the present.

The more you practice NICER, the more seamless it'll become. It's a slow, subtle process of cultivating awareness so that you can witness your inner experience with a bit more spaciousness, a bit more distance.

REFLECTION QUESTIONS

1. Take a moment to imagine your inner critic. What does it look like? Maybe it's your scared younger self, or maybe it's a character who represents your younger self.

2. Recall a time when your anxious thoughts told you a story that wasn't true. How might those thoughts have been trying to protect you?

Just because it's a thought doesn't mean it's the truth. These thoughts are not me—I am the observer of them.

CHAPTER

Emotions Aren't the Problem

Allowing yourself to feel

You're Not in Trouble

"I'm just so . . . I'm just so *angry*," I said to my boyfriend. My mom was asleep on a blow-up mattress on the floor of our studio apartment. I whispered so as not to wake her, and my voice shook with both fire and fear.

"How could this happen again?"

I had just graduated college early to save money, and while I was getting closer to myself, I felt worlds away from my parents. I'd call them most days and the phone would ring and then go to voicemail. It was an abrupt change, but it also wasn't. The emotional distance between us had just changed forms now that I was entering early adulthood. I'd ask them why they were being so distant, and I was met with indirect excuses. I didn't understand what was happening; I just knew it felt horrible.

"I want to visit you," my mom said to me one day when I got through to her. "Just me. I'm going to take the train up and spend the weekend with you."

I was thrilled. In our twenty-two years together on earth thus far, I had so few memories of just the *two* of us. The thought of it felt sacred. When I was growing up, we never had the mom-daughter dates that I watched my friends have. One of the few memories I have of just the two of us is me sitting next to her on the couch, watching *The Golden Girls*, before I walked myself to elementary school. So, this trip was special. We picked a date, she booked her train ticket, and I planned a weekend-long itinerary.

When the day arrived, I went to Penn Station to welcome her at the top of the escalator. When I finally saw her curly, graying red hair peeking out along the sliding stairs, it was hard to believe what I was seeing. *My mom was visiting* me. *Just us.* We hugged tightly, her head landing at my armpit, and I grabbed her suitcase and began to lead her toward the part of Penn Station where the subways come in.

"Are you hungry? We could grab lun—" I turned around, and she was gone. Nowhere to be found. I moved in circles, confused. I whipped my phone out of my back pocket and called her. "Meg?"

She answered on the first ring. "I'm lost."

"Lost? Mom, what are you talking about? What do you see around you?" After minutes of frantic cry-shouting and exchanging descriptions of our surroundings, I found her, and it hit me. In the months when my calls had been ignored, my mom's Alzheimer's had gotten worse. For the past couple of years, she had been steadily declining at a slow pace, but because we never talked about it openly as a family, I'd had no idea it had gotten this bad. We went to the kiosk to get her a subway card, and I realized that she had stepped onto the train with only an expired credit card and a crumpled twenty-dollar bill in her wallet.

We made it back to my apartment and dropped her bags. She took my hand in hers. "I'm so happy to be here, Meggy," she said. We agreed that fresh air would do us good, so we strolled along the water at Battery Park, I pointed out the Statue of Liberty from afar, and we decided we'd get five-dollar tacos around the corner for dinner. *This feels normal. This feels nice*, I thought.

The next morning, my mom was pacing around the studio in her nightgown, muttering to herself. "Everything okay?" I asked on my way to the bathroom.

"Yeah, it's just, I haven't heard from your father since I got here."

My stomach dropped, immediately knowing, but not wanting to.

"Let's go for a walk," I said.

This had happened with my dad the one other time she had tried to visit me, and it was happening again: he drank, he drove, he got caught, and he needed to be bailed out. In dreadful silence, we puttered along the cobblestones of the Seaport. We both knew what had happened, but who would dare to say it first? She would cut her trip short to go back and tend to the dogs, who were home alone.

"Don't leave," I begged her. "Why not just finish your trip and we can get someone to look after the dogs?"

"I know, Meggy. I'm so sorry. I have to go."

I booked her a new train ticket and took her to Penn Station the next day. I texted her every thirty minutes on her ride back to make sure she was okay and then asked our neighbor to stay with her at the house while we figured this out. It was the last time she'd ever visit me.

After she left, my dad started calling me multiple times a day, asking me to help get him out of jail, to figure out a plan. That's what daughters do. Daughters handle it. I'm the youngest child but the only daughter, so I might as well be the oldest child. He said

115

he'd start calling me more often once this was all over, and I believed him, because there was still a sliver of hope within me that he was telling the truth. *In his life when he needs me, out of his life when he doesn't.*

"You can be angry," my boyfriend said to me. "I get it now. You're allowed to be angry."

That familiar sinking feeling from childhood visited me once again: anger bubble-wrapped in shame. *Does being angry make me a bad daughter? My parents are suffering, too. I shouldn't be upset.* But blanketing my anger in shame didn't make the anger disappear—it just made it more complicated. *I'm allowed to feel angry*, I thought to myself. *I'm not in trouble this time.*

As a teenager and as a young adult, I feared that I was a chronically angry person, but I began to see how not chronically angry I was since I'd been living on my own. To my surprise, I was quite happy a lot of the time. It was the environment and the situations I was put in that elicited so much anger within me.

If feeling anger made me a "bad girl," then so be it—because it turned out being a "bad girl" just meant listening to how I was feeling and letting those feelings be okay. It turned out being a "bad girl" just meant being honest with myself about what I was able to do and how much I was able to give. That was what I was guilty of.

Maybe for the first time ever, I let myself feel anger without shaming myself for it.

There Are No Bad Emotions

When I hear the term "negative emotions," I find myself flinching a little. I prefer to call them "uncomfortable" or "challenging" emotions. These emotions may be accompanied by sensations in the body that are unpleasant, but that doesn't mean the emotions are *bad*.

With the fawn response, it was protective for you to hyperfocus on what others were feeling and therefore lose the connection that you had with your own internal world. If you remained totally focused on making sure other people were happy and managing their moods, you didn't get the opportunity to know the vastness of your emotions and how to coexist with them.

How you relate to your emotions is a window into (1) how your caregivers related to *their own* emotions and (2) how they related to *your* emotions when you were growing up.

It makes sense that so many of us learned to think of certain emotions negatively. If we witnessed our caregivers' emotions seeming out of control, we naturally learned that it was unsafe to be with someone who was feeling angry, sad, annoyed, anxious—and to manage their emotions as a way to return to safety.

And if our caregivers couldn't manage or hold their own emotions within themselves, they would react to our emotions the way they internally related to *their* emotions. So then we learned: *When I feel anger, or sadness, or other emotions, it makes people upset. It causes conflict. Love is taken away from me, or my emotions are completely ignored. I receive the most love and care when I'm happy, so*

117

I need to be happy all the time in order to feel safe. And when I feel "bad" emotions, I need to shove them down.

So we never learn how to live with these uncomfortable—and human—emotions. We may pretend that everything is okay even when it's not, because we have learned that there's no space for our emotions and something is wrong with us if we feel them. It's never too late to reteach ourselves to be with our emotions, to honor them and allow them to be there.

Fawning Is Trying to Keep Us from Feeling Uncomfortable Emotions

Fawning, in many ways, is an unconscious attempt to protect ourselves from feeling emotions that are uncomfortable. When you notice yourself fawning in a situation in which you don't need to be, ask yourself: *What emotion am I trying to protect myself from?* Usually, it's an uncomfortable one.

If we're fawning, we won't need to feel the guilt that arises when we set a boundary. If we're fawning, we won't need to feel the fear that may arise when we sit down to have an honest conversation. So much of this healing, then, is slowly and safely increasing our ability to experience discomfort and to identify that as what it is. It's just discomfort—and you can survive discomfort. Healing is the practice of slowly getting comfortable with being uncomfortable. Because we're hardwired to resist discomfort, we tend to jump right into control as a way to avoid the emotion itself. Instead of *How can I fix this?* we can ask ourselves, *What part of me is feeling discomfort from this?*

When they start processing the pain that has been hidden beneath the surface, many clients say, "What am I doing wrong? I'm feeling sadness and anger and fear!"

"Good," I tell them. "You feel safe enough in your body now to be able to feel. And not only are you feeling, but you're able to identify what you're feeling."

Remove the Extra Layer of Criticism

"What's wrong with me? Why am I feeling this way?" Brianna presses her palms against her cheeks like she's trying to empty the air out of them. "I shouldn't be feeling this."

Brianna's angry at herself for feeling angry at her friend.

"Is being angry at the anger making the anger go away?" I ask her.

"No, now I'm just double-angry."

Perhaps one of the most significant roots of our internal suffering is our tendency to judge ourselves for what we're feeling. (Unsurprisingly, we usually judge ourselves only for the uncomfortable emotions.) The inner voice says, *What's wrong with me? When will this go away? I shouldn't be feeling this way!* This makes sense. This voice is trying to protect us from feeling emotions that once got us in trouble or resulted in love being withheld. The mind wants to have control over any emotion that feels uncomfortable to protect us from it, and so we resist and criticize ourselves as a way to feel in control.

The mind thinks: *Maybe if I rip myself apart for being angry and wish that my anger wasn't there, I won't be angry anymore.* If that worked, we'd all be *very* stable by now. But when we judge ourselves for feeling an emotion, the emotion doesn't go anywhere. We now have the emotion *plus* self-criticism and shame and anger. It's an extra layer of tension. We tend to compound our emotions this way. We feel guilty for feeling angry. We feel ashamed for feeling anxious. The emotion itself (fear, for example) is allowed to be here—this is the primary emotion. The stuff we add on top of it—*Why am I feeling this? When will this go away?*—is the secondary emotion, which is the unnecessary layer that prolongs our inner tension.

Very often this extra layer of emotion is an unconscious attempt to cover up the primary emotion, which tends to be more powerful and raw. Rage, for example, can be an attempt to protect us from deep grief and sadness. What a relief it is to (1) notice that this is happening and (2) practice removing the added layer of unnecessary criticism and simply allow the primary emotion to be there, knowing it'll soon pass.

A dear client of mine once said to me, "I spent so many years trying to fix myself and control my emotions, and it turns out that the most impactful thing has just been allowing whatever I'm feeling to be there."

Self-judgment isn't the same as self-inquiry. Saying to ourselves, *Why am I feeling this way? Hmmm. Let's look further* is different from asking, *WHY AM I FEELING THIS WAY? WHAT'S WRONG WITH ME?* The motivation for self-inquiry comes from awareness and curiosity, instead of judgment and urgency. With self-criticism, the motivation comes from control, from wanting to manage our inner experience and "fix" it. It comes from a place of self-loathing. Notice if you're criticizing yourself for criticizing yourself. Remember, that's just the same voice talking to itself.

Frozen in Time

When we've experienced trauma, whether it was a singular major event or unmet needs over a longer time, that younger version of ourself is frozen in the past and still living within us now. In *The Body Keeps the Score*, author Bessel van der Kolk says, "The past is alive in the form of gnawing interior discomfort."[1] When we experience trauma, the protective part of ourself is frozen in that traumatic time and thinks the past is still happening. This protective part still thinks we're six years old, twelve years old, and so on. Even if the trauma occurred long ago, when we're reminded of it, we'll react with the stress of that time because our body thinks it's occurring now.

Let's say you're in a healthy relationship with your partner, and you're in the car together and they're being kind of quiet, so you immediately think, *I've done something wrong. He's mad at me.* In that moment, your body is brought back to the period in your life when silence *did* mean something was seriously wrong. It's like your body is time-traveling back to that experience, remembering your fear and panic and what you needed to do to feel okay again (e.g., soothe the other person, fixate on what you did wrong, or fawn in some other way). Even though fawning may not be necessary to your survival now, in this moment your younger self is coming to the forefront to fix the situation.

In other words, trauma can "freeze" your emotional response at the age when you experienced the trigger most deeply. And because it probably wasn't safe for you to process that experience and those emotions at the time, this younger version of you, frozen in time, is unconsciously dictating your reactions and behaviors. It's not that you're stuck at that age but that you're acting out the emotional wounding that *happened* at that age. Healing the fawn response means being present when your body thinks you're in the past.

Pause—Separate the Emotion from the Reaction

"But what do you mean there's no such thing as a negative emotion? I saw my dad be angry all the time. How is that not negative?" Reese once said to me. This is a fair question that comes from a common misconception.

It's important to separate the *emotion* from the *reaction to the emotion.*

An emotion is the inner experience; it's a physical and mental state, paired with thoughts and bodily sensations. Anger, for example, may create tension in the body, maybe some heat in the chest, constriction in the throat. And maybe anger is saying: *This is really bothering me. Something about this isn't sitting right.* How we *react* to the emotion—the behavior we engage in—that's what's in our control, and that's our responsibility.

During Reese's childhood, her dad would feel anger and then immediately react to the anger in a rageful way—yelling, slamming doors, throwing things across the room. That was his *reaction to the anger.* That was the behavior he engaged in.

The emotion you feel is valid, but that doesn't mean the behavior is.

There's one thing that lies between the emotion and our reaction to the emotion: a pause.

For many of us who are living in a dysregulated state, the emotion and the reaction happen so quickly and chaotically, it feels like one instantaneous process. They blend together. But as we strengthen our awareness and begin to observe what's happening internally, we see that they are two different processes.

First there's a trigger or stimulus, then an emotion and an immediate reaction to the emotion. When we insert a pause, we're creating a small break after the trigger in which we can choose to respond instead of react. This pause is an opportunity to acknowledge the emotion we're feeling without immediately reacting to it. In this pause, we have the opportunity to decide whether we want to continue an old pattern or start a new one.

The immediate reaction is unconscious, and it's often a window into our past, into our habitual reactions. A response is conscious: it's what we're choosing *now*.

We have the choice of staying with the familiar (an unconscious move) or stepping into the inner freedom that exists in the unfamiliar (a conscious move). When we're stuck in a fawn response, we're going to *react* because our bodies think we're in the past and so are acting from a place of survival. When we insert a pause, we're naturally communicating to our bodies that we're safe because there's no time for a pause when we're actually in danger.

This work is not about controlling our emotions; it's about managing our reaction *to* the emotions and bringing awareness to our experiences. Trying to change or erase an emotion doesn't make it go anywhere. By shifting our focus to how we react to the emotion, we give the power back to ourselves.

We're still going to sometimes get triggered and hungry and overstimulated. Reacting to our emotions sometimes is inevitable, and when we react, we don't need to berate ourselves for it. The most important part of any sort of rupture is the repair that comes after the fact: acknowledging our reaction and being curious about it, owning up to it, and taking action to soothe ourselves in the future. This isn't a practice of perfection; it's a practice of compassion.

Emotions Are Messages

Emotions are temporary visitors. Messengers. The neuroscientist Jaak Panksepp defined emotions as "inherited ancestral tools for living."[2] These emotions are not *you*; they're visiting you with little pieces of information. Even the English language intertwines us with our inner experiences. We say, "I am anxious," as if we, as people, are the physical manifestation of anxiety. When we're feeling an uncomfortable emotion, it's human for our mind to zoom in on that emotion and say, *Well, this is me. If I'm angry right now, that means I'm an angry person.* We resist an emotion that's inherently temporary and is trying to pass through us, and we end up prolonging the emotion by trying to control it. Instead of treating our emotions as things to be muted, we can ask ourselves: *What is this emotion communicating to me? What am I needing right now?*

Emotions are messages . . .

ANGER SAYS: My values are being compromised. There's an injustice here. My needs aren't being met. When anger is swallowed again and again, it becomes resentment. Anger can also be protecting us from another emotion, like fear, sadness, or grief.

FEAR SAYS: Something about this feels threatening. My safety or sense of security is being compromised. It may just feel scary because it's unfamiliar, but let's inquire further.

DISAPPOINTMENT SAYS: There's a gap between my expectations, assumptions, or beliefs and what I'm seeing in reality. Whether or not these expectations were realistic, this disappointment is letting me know that what I'm experiencing isn't what I was hoping to experience.

ENVY SAYS: They have something that I would like for myself. This is nudging at a deep desire I have that hasn't yet been fulfilled.

GUILT SAYS: I did something bad or wrong. I feel guilty because my behavior violated, or is out of alignment with, my own personal values or standards.

SHAME SAYS: I am bad or wrong. Guilt and shame are closely related, but shame goes deeper. Shame is a more pervasive feeling that I'm inherently flawed or inadequate as a person, leading me to want to hide or withdraw.

Resentment Is So Important, It Gets Its Own Heading

If there's one emotion I want you to get to know most when healing the fawn response, it's resentment. Resentment is what happens when we've ignored anger again and again, and so it builds up, festers, and gnaws at our bodies. Resentment is the magical little messenger that can support us in determining whether we're fawning (resentment is present) or just genuinely being kind (there's no resentment).

When there *is* resentment, first we can practice just noticing that it's there. And then we can get curious about it: *Do I have a need that isn't getting met? Is there something I need to communicate to let the other person know what I'm experiencing?* Resentment is gold in terms of understanding your needs. Celebrate when you notice resentment. This is a sign that you're listening, a sign that you're reconnecting to the internal world you've been disconnected from for so long.

Not Every Emotion Has to *Mean* Something

Emotions carry messages, yes, but they don't always need to *mean* something. The mind creates stories out of temporary feelings— that's what it does.

The emotion you're feeling is valid, but the story the mind creates about the feeling isn't always true.

Amy's been feeling distant from her longtime partner in their overall very healthy, balanced relationship. They've both been working late hours, running out the door in the morning with barely enough time for a kiss goodbye, and, when they're home, they've been idly existing in the same space like they're just room-mates. The feeling Amy is experiencing is loneliness. The story that Amy's mind is telling her is *Okay, I guess this means our relation-ship is doomed and we should probably just break up because he must not love me anymore. This is horrible. I knew he'd lose interest in me eventually. Who will get the dog?*

The emotion she's feeling (loneliness) is valid, but the story her mind creates about the feeling—*We're doomed as a couple and I'm destined to be alone forever*—isn't necessarily true. Instead, she can let this emotion simply be information: *Okay, I'm feeling distant.* This is good information that she and her partner are in need of some quality time together, some uninterrupted time carved out of their schedules to be with each other. This is an indicator that Amy is craving closeness and connection.

Often the emotions we feel are simply reflections of the im-permanence of every aspect of our lives. It's also normal for us, as humans, to have dips in our closeness in relationships, in our mo-tivation and energy. Perhaps what you're feeling is just a natural part of that cycle. If the emotion is starting to become a recurring *pattern*, it's something to inquire about and pay attention to. Even then, we can have curiosity about the habitual emotion without getting lost in the story of what it must mean.

So many of us understand the *why* of our behaviors and patterns but struggle to process the emotions behind them. This is why the practice of being in our bodies is so important. Constantly intellectualizing and analyzing our emotions is a way of keeping ourselves from really feeling them. It's a protective mechanism: if we're always thinking *about* our emotions and analyzing them, we won't need to physically feel the pain or discomfort that's behind the rationale. When we find ourselves getting lost in the headiness of an emotion and stuck in the story, it's an invitation to return to the bodily experience of that emotion, from the neck down, if it feels safe and accessible to do so. Not everything we feel has to be explained or rationalized. It can just be what we're feeling—without the story. It can just be experienced.

Emotions Are Temporary When We Let Them Be

Uncomfortable emotions have a strange, powerful ability to convince us that the discomfort they bring will last forever. When I recall some of the moments in my life that were emotionally the hardest, I remember thinking: *This will never go away. This is just what my life will be forever.* And now, when I look back on those moments, they feel like distant, vague memories.

Physiologically, emotions have a life span of ninety seconds. Jill Bolte Taylor, a brain scientist from Harvard University, explains that "when a person has a reaction to something in their environment, there's a ninety-second chemical process that happens in the body; after that, any remaining emotional response is just the person choosing to stay in that emotional loop."[3]

This isn't to say that we need to rush through our emotions or force them away if they're not out of our bodies in ninety seconds or less. It's to say, when we're present with our emotions, to the best of our ability, the emotions are inherently temporary. Think of emotions like waves: emotions rise and, therefore, so do the bodily sensations or the discomfort, and then the emotion crashes. It may rise quickly again, or the water may settle for some time.

When we can practice (key word: "practice") acknowledging our emotions without getting stuck in the stories around them, we're in a more grounded place to receive any information they may have for us. The irony is that when we resist our emotions because we think they're unproductive, we end up prolonging them. We're stuck in the feeling for *so much longer* than if we had just allowed ourselves to pause with the emotions and let them move through us.

Pain, naturally, sucks us into it. Reminding ourselves that an emotion is temporary doesn't mean it's any less uncomfortable, and knowing the emotion is impermanent doesn't always make the experience of it feel better. But reminding ourselves that uncomfortable emotions are temporary allows us to say, *Yeah, this is really hard*, and lets that be okay, because we no longer *are* the pain; we are just experiencing it.

Sitting Versus Sulking

There was once an eight-month construction project going on directly outside my apartment window; bulldozing, excavating, and jackhammering went on from six in the morning until six at night. I would walk over to my window to see if the project was magically over, exhale in frustration, and shake my head in disbelief that construction could possibly be happening on a New York City street. Shocking, really. Yes, the annoyance was valid and made sense—*and* I was making it much worse for myself. I was seeking it out, pressing my nose to the window, and muttering under my breath. I refused to put on headphones or use earplugs to block out the staccato *beep beep beep*s and dizzying *whhhiiiiirrr*s from the drills, as if by enduring the noise I would make it go away sooner. The noise wasn't coming to me—I was going to *it*.

There's a fine line between sitting with an emotion and sulking in it, between being with an emotion and becoming it. The difference is similar to my noise-sensitivity debacle. The question is: *Are you searching for the emotion or is the emotion coming to you? Are you seeing a sprout pop up from the dirt, or are you digging it out?*

Of course, sometimes a little slow digging is necessary, like if something that hasn't been addressed is burrowing deep in the crevices of our subconscious mind and we want to bring it to the surface safely and slowly to finally let it be seen. Sulking is when it's no longer an active emotion, alive in our bodies, but instead a scenario playing out in our minds, such that we're no longer feeling anger manifest as heat in our chests and clenching in our throats but we're still stuck in the same loop of the same imaginary argument we've had seven times.

Using "Nicer" to Process Our Emotions

We can use NICER to process our emotions, allowing our awareness to anchor us in the experience of our bodies and draw our attention away from the stories of the mind. When we can be grounded in ourselves as we're experiencing emotions, we give ourselves the spaciousness to pause and respond instead of react. After years of being disconnected from our feelings, the first step is simply acknowledging the emotion.

Notice that an emotion is coming up for you. This is an important, daily practice of observing when an emotion is arising and allowing yourself to say, *This is just what I'm feeling.*

Invite the emotion to be there for a second, like you're welcoming an old friend. You're not clinging to the emotion and you're not resisting it, but rather you're allowing it to be there without shoving it out the door.

Get Curious about the emotion: *What is it that I'm feeling? Is this anger? Resentment? Fear? Okay, and how is this emotion showing up in my body? Do I feel any sensations? Tightness? Heat? Is this emotion communicating something to me, a need that isn't being met?*

Embrace the emotion. Say something like, *Hello, anger, you're allowed to be here. What I'm feeling makes sense. It's safe to feel this.*

Return to what's real and true right now. What do you see around you? Can you feel your breath in your body?

Now, let's be real: we don't always have time to sit with our emotions when we're out in the world. Say you're on a team-wide Zoom call and your boss takes credit for something that you were up until 2:00 a.m. working on. You feel an immediate rush of heat to your face, you feel your heart rate go up, your mind starts to fantasize about quitting on the spot, and you picture yourself saying, "Remember my name. You'll be sorry!" as you rip up a piece of paper (it was actually blank) and make a dramatic exit. If only you could say, "Give me a second, I think I'm feeling anger but let me just go ahead and process it," and then mute your boss while you talked to the anger. That'd be sweet, but no. Not always possible.

In those moments when you're out in the world and don't have five minutes to pause, you can still Notice that you're feeling something, that something has shifted internally for you.

Let's rewind to that call with your boss. They take credit for your work, but you still have to smile, nod, and be professional, and you will probably need to unmute yourself in a second to contribute to the conversation. But in those first three seconds alone, you can simply be conscious of the fact that *something* has changed for you internally, even if you're not sure what.

Later, when you get off the call, you may have more space to re-hash what happened and let yourself acknowledge the anger more deeply. Mindfulness is about accepting reality, and if the reality is that you don't have the time or space to take a few quiet moments with yourself right away, then that's something to be accepted, too. Mindfulness is about being flexible with what's happening right now and being connected to your inner world while engaging with the outer world.

Your mindfulness practice is happening all the time: when you're driving to work, when you're eating leftovers, when you're washing the dishes. It's just paying attention, noticing what's happening right here, right now. No matter what you're doing or where you are, there's always a practice available to you. And even so, mindfulness doesn't mean that we need to be fully present all the time. We won't be; we can't be. Mindfulness is noticing that we're feeling lost in thought, we're dysregulated, we're disconnected, we're ungrounded—and acknowledging that that's happening, too.

Labeling
What Is This?

We can also practice simply labeling our emotions as they arise. Not as a way to intellectualize each emotion but as a way to acknowledge the feelings instead of immediately pushing them away. I'll often do this in my meditation practice, when I'm sitting on my cushion and listening as the little inner voice spews out thoughts about the emails I need to respond to. This voice feels I must end my meditation *right this instant* to respond to those emails or else the world will end. As a way to simplify the noise, I'll say, *This is restlessness,* or *This is anxiety,* or *This is agitation,* or *This is boredom,* or *This is unpleasant.*

Notice how sensations change, how they fluctuate, ebb and flow. Imagine watching a lava lamp. The contents of the lamp are in motion, but the lamp itself, the container, is still.

REFLECTION QUESTIONS

1. What's your current relationship to uncomfortable emotions like anger, sadness, and fear? How do you usually deal with them?

2. Recall a recent time when you felt resentment. What was it telling you?

I am allowed to feel this emotion. Nothing is wrong with me for feeling this. I acknowledge my emotions and allow them to move through me.

CHAPTER

This Is Exhausting

How fawning affects the body

The Body Remembers

My body knew I was fawning before I did. For nearly four years in my early twenties, my throat burned. Constantly. Acid from my stomach was pouring up through my esophagus and into the back of my throat. I wasn't eating any of the foods that usually trigger reflux. I exercised regularly. I wasn't drinking. And yet popping antacids like gumdrops did nothing for me. I was already feeling very anxious and not understanding that what was happening in my body was making me even more anxious, which made the symptoms worse.

It wasn't until I noticed what was happening in my body and began relaxing the muscles in my stomach, breathing deeply, and releasing my grip that my symptoms began to settle. As I started to heal emotionally, my body did, too. As I began to feel safe again, my body got the cue that it was as well. I know now that the burning in my throat was all the swallowed words, the fiery anger that I hadn't allowed myself to feel. The countless instances of using my precious words to overapologize instead of speak up about my needs. After years of inner tension, after years of ignoring intuitive nudges and whispers, my body started to scream.

For most of my life, I was a floating head loosely attached to a body, disconnected from the messages, sensations, and wisdom that existed below my neck. I lived in my mind, and racing thoughts were my resting place. It wasn't until I started to realize what was happening in this home that I had neglected that I began to see how it had been trying to talk to me all along.

The first time I began to wonder about the mind-body connection was in my junior year of high school. Within a two-month period my dad had another Big Relapse, the most damaging one yet, and I found out my long-term boyfriend cheated on me. At the time, both of these events felt earth-shattering and were never addressed. In the months to follow, I'd stand in front of the mirror, combing my fingers through my hair, collecting clumps of it between my fingers. I went to the doctor and told her I was losing my hair.

"Oh, I think you look great!" she said, and waved me off.

When I insisted that it was *really* falling out, she asked if I had been through anything stressful recently. I paused and considered. "No, not really," I said. And I truly believed that at the time. No one in my family was talking about what was happening, so I didn't think it mattered or should have an impact on me. That would've meant it was real. Over the next few months, I lost nearly a third of my hair.

During this period I felt confused and betrayed, as if perfectionism had failed me and something was, in fact, wrong with me. So I sought control through silent self-destruction. I monitored every ingredient that touched my tongue and forced myself to run more miles than my knees could handle, with the fantasy that inner peace would appear if there was a big enough gap between my thighs. If I could control my body, I thought, I could control the emotional pain that was bubbling within it.

I knew it was a problem when I realized my fingers were typing into Google "How many calories are in a teaspoon of vanilla extract?" I told myself it was just out of curiosity, but it was out of habit. Having an unhealthy relationship with food and exercise was so trippy because I kept getting compliments on how I looked. So I thought I had to keep up what I was doing, but I knew I couldn't for long. The irony is that the time when my inner critic said I looked my "best" on the outside was also when I was struggling the most internally.

By the time I unpacked my bags in my college dorm room freshman year, I had started to heal my relationship with food and exercise. But now I found control by losing control, blotting everything out. I was all-or-nothing about drinking. I was either not drinking or blacking out without intending to; there was no in-between. But this pattern seemed normal because everyone got drunk at 2:00 p.m. on a Saturday. I was still diligent about food and exercise—bouncing on the elliptical at 7:00 the morning after, holding back hangover nausea. So I was in control, right? Lose control, gain control. That was the pendulum that I was swinging on, until I got a concussion and I had to just . . . stop. I stopped drinking, and I no longer had the option to run ten miles a day because I could barely walk for ten minutes without needing to nap.

I slowed down, and I felt the anxiety that was there all along. My concussion was indeed quite serious. It would take nearly a year to heal and would be followed by plenty of setbacks in the years to follow. It was during this time of being catapulted back into my body that the anxiety manifested in a different way. I fixated on any and every sensation in my body and convinced myself I was suffering from something terminal. It became a vicious cycle in which anxiety was causing physical symptoms like numbness in my limbs and tingling in my hands and fatigue in my bones, but Google told me that meant I had a brain tumor and I should seek medical attention immediately, and *OMG, I AM GOING TO DIE*, so the anxiety got worse, and the symptoms got worse, and I was trapped in the lies of my mind.

Between the ages of seventeen and about twenty-four, I felt like something was always "wrong" in my body. Hypervigilance toward the outside world—*Are they mad at me? Did I say the wrong thing?*—was bleeding into my inner world: *Why is my arm tingling? What does this mean?!* The ailments popped up like the moles in Whac-A-Mole. Once one issue resolved, another one appeared—gut issues, chronic muscle aches, tension headaches—and these symptoms and figuring out what they meant became my obsession. I was on a mission to figure out what was "wrong" with me, but maybe my physical symptoms were just mirroring what I was feeling internally: that something must be deeply, inherently wrong with me; that who I was, in this body, was wrong and had to be fixed.

I now know that most of these symptoms were mostly related to stress and inflammation and I had to slowly connect to my body in order to heal it. Maybe the ailments served a protective function, to distract my attention from the uncomfortable, unsettling emotions that had lingered within my body for over two decades. I realized that my body wasn't a coffin for my pain and unprocessed emotions. It was a vessel for my life, and I needed to lift the deep pain within me and give it another place to go, to allow it to move through me, out of me, and let it live somewhere else.

Over the following years, changing my relationship to my anxious thoughts, to my body, and to the sensations that swirled around in my body was what gradually expanded my focus. I slowed my body down. I connected to my body and my breath. I started to pay attention to what was happening internally and began to face the discomfort that had been there all along.

Fawning disconnects us from our bodies, and so does living in a society that teaches us to be at war with our bodies—to shrink, make ourselves smaller and slimmer, so we won't be able to take up enough space to fulfill our potential. We're lured into a world of detachment from our bodies to increase the profit of companies that thrive off our self-loathing. It's an act of rebellion against the system when you become *embodied*—in harmony with your body, nurturing it and accepting it in all its seasons, cycles, and fluctuations—because that means you don't need to be smaller, younger, or different to have value. It means you have value right now, as you are.

I've said this before and I'll say it again: healing is slow and subtle. During my first semester of graduate school I was sitting cross-legged on the floor of our studio apartment, half working on a paper, half chitchatting with my husband about how our days had gone. After a pause in the conversation, he said, "How are you feeling, by the way? Physically, I mean. I feel like you haven't talked about any ailments in a while." I looked up from my computer in stunned silence. "Yeah, I've been feeling fine," I replied, almost scared that, by saying it out loud, I could jinx it. "I guess I don't really think about it anymore."

Western Medicine and the Mind-Body Connection

The Western medical model still presumes a disconnect between the mind and the body, viewing them as two separate entities. There's a doctor for the mind and there's a doctor for the body. Even within the body, there's so much separation: we go to a GI doctor for stomach and intestinal issues and a cardiologist for heart concerns, focusing on the individual parts as opposed to the system as a whole. Of course, *sometimes this is necessary.* But it's imperative that we acknowledge how stress and trauma impact both our bodies and our minds.

Sixty to 80 percent of primary care visits are stress-related.[1] More recently, research has shown a relationship between unprocessed stress and autoimmune disorders, particularly in women. Nearly 80 percent of autoimmune diseases are diagnosed in women,[2] yet so many women are told, "Just try to relax" or "It's probably just anxiety," with little guidance beyond that. While genetic and hormonal factors certainly play a major role in autoimmune diseases, we must also consider the psychosocial and emotional factors and the toll that silencing both our needs and our emotions takes on the body. A 2015 study published in *Frontiers in Immunology* highlights that chronic stress and suppressed emotions, particularly anger, can contribute to immune system dysfunction and increase the risk of autoimmune disorders because of elevated levels of stress hormones. Not surprisingly, this stress-induced immune dysregulation is especially significant in women, and even more significant for women of color.[3]

In the West, the mind-body connection is a relatively recent subject of research. In the 1960s, the psychiatrist George Solomon studied how people with rheumatoid arthritis had worse symptoms when they were depressed, leading him to investigate how emotions affected inflammation in the body, pioneering the field of psychoneuroimmunology.[4] Around the same time, the physician Herbert Benson studied how meditation affected blood pressure. He was one of the first Western physicians to bring spirituality and the mind-body connection into Western medicine, and he coined the term "relaxation response" in 1975.

Despite this mind-body framework being relatively new in the West, ancient cultures and healing traditions like Ayurveda and Traditional Chinese Medicine have viewed the mind, body, and spirit as one for thousands of years. In Eastern cultures, specifically Traditional Chinese Medicine, it's widely understood that grief is stored in the lungs, which are considered to be the "custodians of grief." It's said that unresolved grief and unprocessed sadness can disrupt lung function, manifesting as shortness of breath, fatigue, and higher susceptibility to colds and asthma. In Afro-Indigenous cultures, healing often begins with a deep connection to ancestors, viewing their wisdom as a potent source of healing, strength, and guidance.[5]

What I'm describing here isn't new, nor is it mine. Eastern, Indigenous, and ancient practices were saying these things and practicing them long before the West had language for them or did research on them.

Why Fawning Is So Exhausting

How can fawning not be exhausting for the body? You mask your true self in social settings. Your brain is on high alert when you don't need to be. You use up so much of your precious energy to overthink, overanalyze, and overextend.

When we're stuck in a fawn response and in survival mode, our bodies are flooded with the stress hormones cortisol and adrenaline.[6] Our bodies think that the lion is right there (even if there's not an actual threat) and are working overtime to try to make sure we're safe. When we're in chronic survival mode, we usually don't realize it because we've been there for so long. It just feels normal, and it might even seem unfathomable to us that other people *don't* feel it.

On emotional and behavioral levels, prolonged survival mode can manifest as a sense of urgency in the body, leading to a low frustration tolerance, a feeling that things need to get done *right now* or something bad will happen. *I need to respond to this text immediately! I have to resolve this conflict pronto!* Survival mode is a state of constantly feeling irritable and being easily overwhelmed and reactive. It's a feeling of being in a rush even if you're not rushing anywhere.

Because of this urgency or in addition to being in survival mode, it's also common to feel very tired all the time. You may be familiar with the term "allostatic load," which is the cumulative burden of chronic stress on your mind and your body. When our bodies are handling such a heavy load of stress and rarely returning to a baseline state of safety, they will take longer to feel like they are being restored and recovering. This is why it can feel like a weekend isn't enough time, that eight hours of sleep isn't enough—because the body has been working so hard, it needs more time and sleep to recover. And yet, it might feel impossible to relax, because the mind is constantly racing with thoughts and the body is swirling with agitation, so we're in this vicious cycle of needing to rest but not being able to. How can we rest if our bodies think we're in danger? Our bodies cannot properly heal while in survival mode.

The Catch-22 of "Listening to Your Body"

A core practice of healing the fawn response is reconnecting with the body in a slow, safe way.

I went to my first yoga class when I was eighteen, and barely a quarter of the way through the class I rolled up my mat and bolted for the door. The teacher probably thought I had peed myself, but the truth was I just couldn't handle the anxiety I felt in my body. This was one of my first times engaging in a body-and-breath practice, and I was overwhelmed with tension and agitation. As the class went on, I felt more and more panicked, and when I realized that everyone else seemed to be in yogic bliss, I panicked more. Walking out of the studio, I felt so much shame, with *What's wrong with me?* repeating in my mind like a prayer.

I know now that at that point in my life, I had so much unprocessed trauma and pain in my body that being still with myself was absolutely intolerable. There were so many emotions I wasn't ready to feel, so many memories I wasn't ready to face, and all that agitation came pouring in the second I slowed down. Whatever you have experienced, from the womb to now, has happened within the same body. Of course your body is holding on to unprocessed pain.

Trauma research has shown that we can't outsmart trauma or think our way out of it. Trauma is stored in the body, and it lingers there until we feel an internal sense of safety.[7] We don't rewire familiar patterns just by talking to ourselves intellectually; we must show our bodies that we're safe by being able to tolerate discomfort, soothing the scared part of ourselves in that discomfort, and absorbing the realization that we are safe right now, in this moment.

We heal by *showing* our bodies that we can be anxious and safe at the same time. We can be *angry* and safe at the same time. We can be *uncomfortable* and safe at the same time. This takes time to learn and practice.

"Just listen to your body" is confusing advice for trauma survivors and for people who've needed to disconnect from their bodies as a means of self-protection. How can we listen to our bodies if it has felt uncomfortable and unsafe to exist in those bodies? How can we listen to our bodies if we never learned to?

This is why *slowly* increasing our tolerance for discomfort is so important to trauma healing. When a client is starting therapy, we don't just dive headfirst into their most traumatic memory. We go slowly, create a safe container for us to be in together, welcome memories when they're ready to arise, and pause if they are too much to handle. In a similar vein, you wouldn't want to endure thirty minutes of meditation if you'd never sat quietly with your body before; you'd want to start with just three to five minutes.

This is what I like to call dipping our toes in discomfort and being able to come back out. When we give ourselves bite-size portions of discomfort, our bodies can properly digest it. If we abruptly and quickly expose ourselves to too much discomfort, it will be a shock to the nervous system and the body will be like, *See? It* is *dangerous to be with myself. This is why I fawn! Take me back to the patterns that I know!* If we were to go too fast too soon, it would feel shocking and unsafe to the body and would reinforce the belief that our emotions must be feared.

Acknowledging Stress Can Ease Its Toll

As we've previously discussed, the body doesn't know the difference between an imagined experience and an actual experience. The same stress hormones are being released in both instances. So when you're zoning out on the couch, imagining a worst-case scenario—like your boss firing you because her Slack message said "ok" instead of "okay!"—your body thinks you're actually getting fired. *How exhausting.*

Yet research has actually shown that our *perception* of stress can significantly affect its impact on our health. In studies, those who perceived stress as helpful had few long-term negative health effects from stress. In other words, when we can notice that stress is happening and not add more stress to it, but rather relate to it as a part that's trying to protect us, it takes less of a toll on our bodies.

Inhale, Exhale

When we are living in survival mode and stuck in the fawn response, our breathing is shallow. We're not taking in much oxygen, our chests are barely rising with each breath. Rewind to when we popped out of the womb: newborns, in their sweet and doughy form, naturally practice diaphragmatic breathing, which means breathing deeply from the muscle below the lungs, the diaphragm. Diaphragmatic breathing is the most natural and most efficient way to breathe. It's what we do when we feel safe and relaxed. But for those of us stuck in the stress response, our breaths are shallow and short—and that has an impact on our emotional and physical well-being.

In moments of stress—whether life-threatening, like being chased down the street, or less life-threatening, like needing to unmute yourself to give a presentation to a sea of fifty unfamiliar faces staring at you, or accidentally sending screenshots of your text conversation *with* your crush *to* your crush instead of to your best friend (no, I've never done this; what are you talking about?)—it's normal for our breathing to become shallow and erratic. Our heart rate goes up; our palms sweat; our muscles tense. These are all parts of the *sympathetic nervous system response*, which is what happens in the body during moments of high stress.

And then the moment passes. You nailed your presentation, you quickly unsent the screenshots—the threat is gone, and you're back to feeling okay(ish). But many of us are in this sympathetic nervous system state most of the time and are stuck in a constant cycle of shallow, erratic breathing. Maybe not to the extent of the ultrahigh stress moments, like being chased down the street, but we're not breathing as deeply as we're meant to.

Over the past few decades, research has shown that full, deep diaphragmatic breathing[8] is connected to a *parasympathetic nervous system response*, which is the state the body goes into when it knows it's safe, there's no threat, and it can relax. The MVP in this process is the vagus nerve, which is a wildly long cranial nerve that runs from your brain to your large intestine. So if we're feeling unsafe, we're not going to breathe fully. *But we can use our breath to communicate to our bodies that we are safe.* When we engage in slow, deep diaphragmatic breathing, the vagus nerve activates the parasympathetic nervous system; the body now knows that it's safe and is cued to focus on necessary functions such as balancing hormones and digesting food properly that keep it running smoothly. When we're stuck in survival mode and *not* breathing fully and slowly, our bodies don't have the energy to concentrate on those other processes.

Chronic shallow breathing can contribute to many issues, such as through tense muscles and gut issues, poor sleep, hormone imbalances, decreased blood flow to major organs, a weakened immune system, and more. When our cells receive an inadequate oxygen supply, it reduces our ability to digest food, creating utter exhaustion in the organs. When we're in survival mode, our bodies can't heal, restore, and balance themselves the way they're supposed to.

In a 2009 review, researchers at Columbia University discussed their finding that slow, deep breathing was associated with reduced stress in groups of people suffering from post-traumatic stress disorder (PTSD) as well as in groups of healthy individuals who were managing everyday stress.[9] Not only that, but the evidence of stress reduction was often immediate—and, over the long term, deep, diaphragmatic breathing has been shown to reduce cortisol levels in the body. Our breath is a brilliant built-in tool that's here to support us in our healing. It's free, and it's always available to us as long as we're alive, no matter where we are, no matter how little time we have. When our bodies are frozen in the past, focusing on our breath affirms that we're actually here, right now. It's how we can communicate to our bodies that we're calm and safe.

Let's try it together: Inhale for 4, exhale for 6. Repeat 3 to 5 times.

Addicted to Stress

Being in chronic survival mode also messes with the brain. When the sympathetic nervous system is always activated (refresher: that's the state we go into when the body thinks there's a threat), it becomes hard for the brain to prioritize anything else; it's focused on looking for imminent danger. Even situations that are supposed to be fun, like social gatherings, can quickly become exhausting because we're unconsciously hyperfocused on people's moods, facial expressions, and perceptions of us. This intense, narrow focus can lead to overwhelm when we are dealing with daily tasks or even making small decisions because the brain is using so much of its energy to identify and eliminate the threat.[10]

It can be so damn hard to break out of the stress cycle—and so challenging to rest when we're in survival mode—because our bodies unconsciously become addicted to the stress. During these times of high levels of stress, the brain releases dopamine, which activates its reward center. And because the brain's job is to protect us from danger, it is like, *Ooooh, sweet, I got a reward! Positive reinforcement! I need to keep being stressed!* This is why, so often, we unconsciously seek out situations that aren't good for us (e.g., high-stress jobs, toxic relationships, and so on). Our bodies have only ever known that level of stress, so they crave it. Remember what we talked about in chapter 2: what feels familiar to the body is going to feel safe.

The body naturally responds to stress—whether it's real, remembered, or perceived—with tension, and this response keeps stress and tension going in a flirty little loop. The process goes a little like this:

STEP 1: Something stressful happens, either internally or externally—an anxious thought spiral or someone doing something to make you feel unsafe, whether or not you actually are.

STEP 2: Your body tenses up.

STEP 3: Tense muscles say to the body: *Something bad is happening! This is stressful!*

STEP 4: The tense muscles cue more anxious thoughts, more muscular tension, and more panic, continuing the cycle of stress and tension.

When the mind is tense, so is the body. When the body is tense, so is the mind. By first *noticing* that we're tensing up, feeling stressed, we can immediately insert a pause into this automatic process and begin to soften our bodies. Being aware of the stress is what allows us to start to break the cycle. Even when we notice it, we may still be stressed and tense! That's okay. Just by being aware of it, we're already doing something new. Remember, the goal isn't to get rid of our challenging emotions but to become more aware of them and then change our relationship to them.

Trauma Is a Time Traveler

The trauma that we're carrying in our bodies isn't just our own. On the physical, emotional, and spiritual levels, we're carrying the unprocessed wounds, unmet needs, and unaddressed trauma of our parents, their parents, and those who came before them. This is intergenerational trauma.

Remarkable studies on intergenerational trauma have shown that adult children of Holocaust survivors—their *children*, not the survivors themselves—had a genetic marker indicating lower cortisol levels than Jewish adults whose parents were *not* in the Holocaust.[11] And when we're evaluating for PTSD, low cortisol levels are a strong indicator. While it may seem counterintuitive that low cortisol levels would occur with PTSD, this is an adaptive response to chronic stress, including intergenerational trauma. It happens because prolonged exposure to stress can lead to dysregulation of the hypothalamic-pituitary-adrenal (HPA) axis, which regulates the body's response to stress. This blunts the cortisol response and lowers the body's baseline amount of cortisol over time. This is to say that the trauma that lives in our bodies is not just about our own lived experiences but also about the tragedies, oppression, and marginalization of the family members who came before us.

The trauma psychologist Mariel Buqué explains that there are two modes of transmission for intergenerational trauma: the first is biology, through expression of genes that are inherited from each parent. If either of the parents experienced trauma that was unprocessed or unaddressed, that can alter the genetic code that gets passed down to their child. The second mode of transmission, perhaps the more obvious one, is psychological behaviors, practices, neglectful patterns, and conflict avoidance.[12]

While the West is just beginning to acknowledge the impact of intergenerational trauma, ancient cultures understood how trauma was passed down long before modern medicine had the language to describe it and the research to understand it. "Our Elders have always said, 'What we do today will affect the next seven generations,'" says integrative healing therapist and Métis/Cree Indigenous elder Kerrie Moore.[13] "Repetitive traumas that happened to our ancestors as many as seven generations before can be passed down to our children."

Researchers have found significant disparities in the experience of trauma between those of different races and ethnicities.[14] Among White, Black, Hispanic, and Asian populations, Black individuals had the highest rates of PTSD. The prevalence of trauma in Black communities is systemic and systematic. The study of intergenerational trauma illuminates how individuals experience the effects of structural, institutional, and interpersonal racism through time and space. Research on epigenetics (the study of how behaviors and environment can alter our gene expressions) has shown that what was traumatic or threatening to one generation can activate or deactivate certain genes, which then get passed down through DNA. These can be specific singular events or they can be widespread cultural trauma that's embedded in the oppressive systems we live in.

We know that our own stress can activate or deactivate these genes and thus be passed down through our DNA, and so can our healing. Healing our own trauma is always possible; in doing so, we're breaking the cycle of generations of trauma.

Pain travels through families until someone is ready to face it.

There's a profound mystery to intergenerational trauma: that it can have such a deep impact on our bodies and nervous systems even though we may not have been alive or conscious of that trauma when it happened, and we may not have family members to tell us what happened. Intergenerational trauma is not always something we can point to and say, "Oh! This is what happened to me." There's grief, and there's also surrender. There's no room for intellectualizing our trauma if we don't have a memory of it. We can't always know what happened to us, and we don't need to know in order for us to heal. We can use our present-day experiences as an indication of what younger versions of ourselves, or our ancestors, may have gone through.

Softening the Body, Slowing the Body

In this work, you'll find that repetition is very important. Every day, we have the opportunity to practice being connected to ourselves. Maybe even right now, as you're reading this, you can soften your stomach. Maybe you can lower your shoulders a little bit and release any tightness in your throat.

We live in a world that demands much of us all the time, at a fast pace. Sometimes this pace can be necessary and inevitable, such as when we have a hard deadline at work or need to pay rent on the first of the month. At other times, this sense of urgency isn't necessary or even helpful. We carry this urgency into our relationships when we don't need it, like when we feel pressure to text someone back right away or to pick up their call even if we're not up for it. We also carry the urgency into other aspects of our day, like when we gobble up dinner, inhaling each bite in a blur as if our lives depend on it. The greatest irony is that often this urgency overwhelms our bodies and we can end up doing . . . nothing. We're sent into a state of inner paralysis in which even the smallest things feel daunting. And the cycle continues.

While we're in survival mode, this urgency convinces us that in order for us to feel better, we just need to try harder and think smarter and do more. But self-regulation happens when we meet this urgency with slowing down. When we focus on slowing down, we actually have a greater ability and a higher capacity to get things done, because our bodies feel safe enough to focus. We need to slow down to speed up.

There's simplicity in cutting out the noise of what you're "supposed to do" and focusing first on slowing down and listening for what you need.

Will was deep in survival mode after years of unprocessed childhood trauma. Growing up in a critical home that overly valued achievement, he learned that he constantly needed to be doing more and going faster in order to be enough. In our early sessions, an all-consuming sense of urgency added to the pressure that he felt to "fix" himself ASAP. Through our work, we peeled back this layer to see that underneath the urgency was the belief that he needed to be perfect. But if Will admitted he was healing, that meant he felt damaged, which then meant he wasn't perfect. This contradiction was intolerable for the part of him that was fixated on survival, because growing up, he only ever received love when he was perfect.

When Will was anxious, he'd go on a walk around his neighborhood and then feel angry at himself because he didn't feel completely better. He'd do a ten-minute breathwork video on YouTube and then feel ashamed that he had a hard time focusing. If he were "perfect," he thought, that single video would have done the trick. A large part of our work, then, was releasing the pressure that he put on himself to heal.

"What if these practices were just about feeling 1 percent better?" I said.

He paused at that, his shoulders softening a little bit. "Yeah, that's much more doable."

By slowly unraveling the belief that these small everyday practices were supposed to be *big* things, Will was able to reap their benefits with more ease and without feeling like he was somehow failing. Complex trauma occurs over time, over many micromoments. Healing takes place in the same way. Just as trauma accumulates in the micromoments, bodily regulation happens in the micromoments as well. It happens when you have five minutes before a call and you sit quietly with your breath instead of scrolling on your phone. It happens when you sprinkle three to five minutes of meditation throughout the day instead of forcing yourself through twenty minutes of extreme discomfort. Remember, we want to dip our toes in the discomfort and be able to come back out.

Grounding Practices for the Body

Here are some grounding practices that you might like to scatter through your daily life. Some of these practices may seem annoyingly obvious to you; maybe you've heard of them before. *That's because they work.* The mind tends to want healing to be more complicated than it is. The good news is that the most impactful healing practices happen when we simply focus on grounding the body:

ELONGATE THE EXHALE. Make your exhale longer than your inhale (like breathing in for a count of 4, breathing out for 6). This stimulates the vagus nerve and immediately activates the parasympathetic nervous system.

5 4 3 2 1. Ground yourself in your current environment. Look around and name five things you can see, four things you can feel, three things you can hear, two things you can smell, and one thing you can taste.

I SPY. Gaze around your environment and notice everything that's green—or any other color. (Or notice things that look smooth or bumpy or that are moving.) You may also incorporate movement into this practice by going on a color walk. Choose a color to focus on and look for that color during your walk. You'll notice how quickly your brain starts to find it. This is a simple way to anchor yourself in the present moment when your thoughts are extra chatty.

HUM. Close your mouth, relax your jaw, inhale through your nose, and exhale through your nose, making a sound with your vocal cords. Your voice will create a soft buzzing sound, and this vibration stimulates your vagus nerve. The same is true for singing or chanting, because the larynx, or the voice box, is connected to the vagus nerve.

BE IN NATURE. It almost feels clichéd to say this because so much research shows the grounding effect of immersing ourselves in nature— yet we don't even need research to know that. We feel it. Since our bodies are part of nature, by spending time in nature we're really just returning to ourselves. Access nature in a way that's possible for you. When I was living in New York City, I'd find a patch of grass to lie on at a local park, and I would track the phases of the moon as a way to feel connected.

PLACE YOUR HAND WHERE THE TENSION IS. Studies have shown again and again how effective touch is in alleviating stress, and this benefit also comes from self-touch. Put your hand on your chest when you feel tension there; place your palm on your throat when you feel tightness. Breathe deeply.

BILATERAL STIMULATION. This is a fancy phrase for stimulating both the left and the right side of your brain, which helps to calm the nervous system. We can do this in many ways, but the most accessible is through tapping. Place your hands on your knees when sitting, or cross your arms on your chest so you have a hand on each shoulder, and alternate gently tapping. Left, right, left, right.

VISUALIZE A TIME YOU FELT SAFE. As we now know, the body doesn't know the difference between an imagined experience and a real experience when we're picturing a worst-case scenario. But the same is true for soothing thoughts. Recall a time when you felt safe: Where were you? What did it feel like? Were you with anyone? If it's hard to do this, can you imagine a place where, or a time when, you *would* feel safe and comforted?

LEGS UP THE WALL. This is a yoga pose (*viparita karani* in Sanskrit) known to reverse the body's energy flow and calm the nervous system. Lie down on the floor, scoot your butt as close to the wall as you can, and swing your legs up along the wall as you lie comfortably on your back. Once your legs are along the wall, see if you can scoot your butt even closer to the wall.

MOVE IT THROUGH YOU. Emotions carry energy that wants to move through us. Especially for fiery, jittery emotions like anger or anxiety, moving the body in a way that feels good, such as going for a brisk walk, allows any stagnant emotion to be broken up.

SHAKE IT OFF. Animals instinctively shake after a stressful event as a way to reset their nervous system, but humans often suppress this natural response, causing us to store the trauma in our bodies. By consciously engaging in shaking, we can release some of this stored energy and support our bodies in returning to a state of safety. Find a space that feels safe to you and shake your body, bounce around, flutter your lips, let your limbs go.

DANCE IT OUT. Dancing is a powerful practice for integrating movement and breath. It's hard to be in your head when you're dancing to a song that pulls you into your body.

PUSH AGAINST A WALL. This is my favorite practice for moving anger through me. Face a wall and press your hands against it, pushing firmly. As you're doing this, feel your strength. Exhale it out. Remind yourself, *This anger is allowed to be here.*

DO SLOW STRETCHING. Light a candle, take a few deep breaths, and do some gentle stretching, letting yourself move slowly and softly.

Shifting the Focus

When I was in the depths of my anxiety, a therapist helped me practice cultivating more compassion for my body. When I found myself hyperfocusing on a part of my body that I felt badly about, I would first notice that negativity, allow it to be there, then practice acknowledging what that part of my body did for me: *Thank you, stomach, for allowing me to digest delicious food properly and for preparing my body to get energy from that food. Thank you, arms, for dancing with me, for allowing me to embrace the people and animals I adore. Thank you, legs, for carrying me through my life so effortlessly, for transporting me from one place to the next, for allowing me to move my body and stroll through the forest and walk my groceries up to my apartment on the third floor.*

Every second of every day, our bodies are working endlessly to allow us to live. Consciously choosing to stop being at war with our bodies and instead work with them, thank them, understand them, pay attention to them, and care for them is an intimate act of returning home to the self.

REFLECTION QUESTIONS

1. What's your relationship to your body? Has it felt like a safe place in which to exist?
2. Close your eyes and see if you can notice just one or two sensations in your body. Describe them.

I breathe deeply and fully. When my mind is traveling to the past or the future, my breath is the anchor that returns me to the present.

CHAPTER

Nothing Is Personal

And other terrifying, liberating truths

It's Not You, It's Me

"I felt like he wasn't interested in what I was saying, and it made me feel like I was boring, so I just kept . . . talking. Uncontrollably! It was awful." Anne describes a housewarming party she went to where she was standing by the snack table and started chatting up a tall guy with short patience.

"And what did that bring up for you?" I ask her.

"Oh, nothing. Just that I'm destined to be alone and that no one is ever going to love me," she replies.

We pause together, slowing down.

"Or maybe, just *maybe*, we can sit with the possibility that his lack of interest is proof that he's not the one for you, instead of proof that you're not lovable. If he were the right fit for you, you wouldn't need to work so hard to prove that you're worth loving."

She inhales, then lets out a sigh, considering.

"I've been thinking about what you said last time," she says. "That I overexplain myself and overshare as a way to prevent rejection, an attempt to feel heard, like 'Here's everything about me so if you don't like it, fine, tell me now.' Especially because I didn't feel heard growing up."

"Keep going with that thought," I encourage her.

"Well, I guess my interpretation of his reaction is because I fear it's true. That I'm not lovable." She pauses. "Damn it. I thought I healed that."

—

Many of us fawners have been conditioned to take things personally for our own safety. We learned to rely on external validation to tell us that we're safe and loved, and to then feel worthless when that external validation is taken away, causing us to crave more of it. We internalized others' bad moods as proof that something is wrong with us, using self-blame as an effective coping mechanism to make sense of criticism, neglect, or chaos. This sensitivity was necessary to stay alert in our environment so that we could adapt, whether within the family system or to society as a whole. In other words, *not* taking things personally felt unsafe to some extent because many of us needed to be on high alert when we weren't receiving positive feedback. Neutral or negative feedback was a sign that there was a threat—and that wasn't something that could be ignored.

A Window Into Our Wounds

The things we tend to take personally aren't things to shame ourselves for but are windows into our deepest wounds and fears. They provide a peek into some really rich information about a part of ourselves that's wanting to be soothed and held.

Mikaela, like many fawners, has a fear of being seen as bad, of being seen as an impostor, of being "found out." As a result, she spends much of her energy trying to uphold her perfect image as a way to protect herself from having people see what she believes is the "real" her, someone who's phony and not worth loving. Because of this wound, anytime someone says something that could imply that Mikaela isn't 100 percent perfect, she takes it very personally and is sent into a spiral, convincing herself that now they know the secret that she is, indeed, bad and wrong. Making a small mistake at work quickly turns into believing that her coworkers have found out she's incapable of doing her job. If she tells a joke that doesn't go over well with her friends, she fears they think she's a terrible person. She then feels like she needs to "correct" the perception, to prove to them that she's perfect so she can feel safe again.

Unsurprisingly, being perfect was Mikaela's safety mechanism growing up, so it feels terrifying to her body to veer away from that image. A large part of our work together involved shifting the story away from what other people must think of or believe about her and toward the wound that lingered beneath. Instead of using her energy to berate herself for letting her perfectionism slip, Mikaela worked on learning to soothe the part of her that feared it was bad in the first place.

Not taking things personally doesn't mean that we're stuck in our ways, that nothing we do is wrong and we are perfect and nothing has to change. But we can acknowledge that a pattern or behavior doesn't feel good and seek to alter that pattern or behavior without self-loathing. We can work toward self-improvement without shaming parts of ourselves for it. We can ask ourselves: *What part of me was activated by this and what does this part need?*

And on the flip side, we can notice what we used to take personally and what we no longer do and use these observations to measure how far we've come in our healing. I used to take my dad's reactions and emotional absence so personally. I'd think, *He isn't interested in my life because I'm not lovable. I'm not deserving of having a close relationship.* I know that I've come a long way in my healing because I'm more accepting of this distance and I feel less need to "fix" it in order to prove myself in some way. Instead, my belief has shifted to *This is what it is. This is how close we can be at this time.* It's no longer about me—it just is. This change in my perspective hasn't necessarily shifted anything in the relationship itself; it's a shift within me, a greater acceptance, a greater ability to lean back and not work so hard to change his mind.

The Three P's

In Buddhism, three marks of existence—*anicca*, *anatta*, and *dukkha*—define our human reality. The Buddhist teacher Ruth King translates these characteristics of life as *nothing is personal*, *nothing is permanent*, and *nothing is perfect*.

NOTHING IS PERSONAL

"Don't take it personally" can be annoying advice. That's like saying, "Stop thinking." The brain is always trying to make sense of things, to categorize, to simplify. We often internalize events, interactions, and issues we encounter and magnify the role that we played in them. This is called *personalization*—a cognitive distortion in which we blame ourselves for an event or situation even if it has little or nothing to do with us.

We overestimate our personal responsibility for something, especially when that thing is negative. (Remember, this belief is from a part of our brains focused on survival that's just trying to be prepared for every outcome.) So we end up thinking, at least on an unconscious level, that things are all about us.

Reminding ourselves that nothing is personal is a really challenging practice—and it's an imperfect one. It doesn't mean we can't feel hurt or upset; it just means we're slowing down and stepping back before spiraling into telling ourselves the usual stories. You're allowed to feel an emotion when something is hurtful, and that emotion is valid. You're a human, not a lifeless slab of flesh. The practice is to not immediately believe what the mind deduces from that emotion. You can let an emotion sting without adding an extra layer of self-loathing for feeling hurt or upset.

Yet releasing constant self-blame doesn't mean that we're stripping away any sort of accountability. It doesn't mean we never own up to our mistakes and take responsibility when we've done something wrong. We can acknowledge that there's room for improvement, or a quality we want to work on, without creating bigger stories about our self-worth. We can work to improve our ability to self-soothe and emotionally regulate without it meaning that we're the worst person on this earth and our existence is an inherent problem.

They Probably Aren't
Thinking About You

People aren't thinking about you as much as you may believe. Researchers from Cornell University coined the term "spotlight effect" after finding that people tended to overestimate how much others noticed them.[1] Participants in their study were asked to wear embarrassing T-shirts in public and then estimate how many people noticed and remembered them. The participants consistently overestimated the number of people who noticed their shirts. In other words, people aren't paying attention to you as much as you may think they are—and they're definitely not remembering your cringey moments as vividly as you are. In a similar vein, we tend to overestimate the degree to which our thoughts and emotions are visible to others. This is a cognitive bias called the *illusion of transparency*.[2]

Each person I pass on the street has their own ambitions, worries, friends, crushes, favorite foods, and pet peeves. And while I'm living in my own body, seeing the world through my eyes, feeling like the main character in my life, I might appear only once as an "extra" in someone else's life, walking my dog in the background or driving a car they're passing in traffic. It's a strange feeling, and it's a comforting one.

As humans, we see ourselves as central in our world. We have egos. That's not a good or bad thing—it's just how we operate. We're not trying to rid ourselves of this aspect of our human existence, but we do want to become aware of it and learn to work with it, not against it. I find that when we can practice zooming out from the contents of our minds and remind ourselves that we're all feeling sucked into our own little world, we can care less about how we're being perceived.

You Can't Control Other People's Perceptions

I both hate and love to break it to you: you can't control other people's perceptions of you. Even when you're working overtime in an attempt to control how you're being perceived, the other person is still seeing you through the lens of their own inner world. And by trying to gain control of others' perceptions, you're losing something in the process: your sense of self, your precious energy, your peace of mind. Even if you were to do everything "perfectly" for everyone and cater to their exact personality preferences, you still wouldn't have control over how they perceive you. With fawning, your mind *thinks* it has control over how people are perceiving you, but this is a false sense of control. The truth is that others' perceptions were never in your control. People will judge you, misunderstand you, and hold perceptions of you that you don't agree with. That's okay.

Do They Like Me?

As you heal your fawn response, there will be people who will dislike you. This doesn't mean everyone will hate you. It means that you'll get clarity on the type of person you want to spend time with. You'll know who feeds your energy and who sucks energy out of you. Let it be a positive sign that you're not for everyone. You can't be for absolutely everyone and know yourself at the same time. When someone doesn't like you, instead of asking, *What should I do to make them like me?* you can instead ask, *How can I soothe myself through the discomfort of them not liking me? What do I need to be okay?*

You are not responsible for the version of you that exists in other people's minds. You can't control how others perceive you, but you can manage how much mental space you give their perceptions. You can't control other people's behaviors, but you can control your decision to tolerate them or not.

Cindy's fawn response manifests as a lot of social anxiety. She has a deep fear that she will be perceived as weird, that people will forget about her, that she'll be irrelevant and get left alone, because this was her experience when she was a kid. Her family *did* make her feel like she was weird, and she *was* left alone because of it. To prevent herself from feeling socially anxious, she would isolate herself, which would then prove to that anxious part of her, *You're right! Life is terrifying! You win: let's stay inside.* For Cindy, healing meant showing that anxious part that when she engaged in social interactions, either no one judged her the way she feared they would or they *did* judge her, and she survived it. She's still here! So much of fawning is rooted in a deep fear of abandonment. There's power in seeing that the adult version of abandonment (e.g., someone doesn't like you) has happened and you're still breathing.

A big chunk of my work with Cindy was focused on her acknowledging the reality that sometimes people are mean and do act from a place of judgment, which is out of one's control. Social anxiety is often about feeling unworthy: *I don't deserve to take up space, to be in this room with these people.* Cindy had been isolating herself because she believed her worth was tied to how people were treating her in social interactions, and our work was flipping that narrative: *I know I'm worthy of being loved and respected in a relationship. Let's find people who know that, too.*

But Do *I* Like *Them*?

When you're stuck in the fawn response, you work very hard to make sure everyone likes you, but perhaps the more important question to ask is: *Do you even like the person you're seeking approval from?* It's not that healing fawning means we don't take honest feedback—it means being selective about whom we're taking feedback from.

Having an open heart doesn't mean you need to be friends with everyone.

Ask yourself: *Do I like and respect the person I'm receiving feedback from? Does their opinion genuinely matter to me, or am I internalizing their perception of me from a place of fear? Does this person embody an energy that I admire and want to embody myself?*

If you're constantly analyzing some relationships and not others, it might be worth evaluating whether you feel emotionally safe in those relationships. Does your body tense up when that hot-and-cold friend just "likes" your message but you're totally fine when your steady best friend does the same thing? Is the fawn response activated with the hot-and-cold friend because your body is unsure whether you can trust them? Take inventory of whom you feel emotionally safe with and use that feeling to guide you in determining which relationships you want to invest in. Relationships take work, yes, but the right relationships make that work easier to do.

What if you stopped giving so much to relationships that take too much from you?

What if you stopped trying so hard to prove yourself to people whom you don't even really like?

What if you broke the cycle of trying to make unavailable people available?

What's the worst-case scenario in the event that someone doesn't like you, and how can you survive the discomfort?

Not taking things personally doesn't mean accepting whatever people say and letting it slide in any relationship. It doesn't mean being detached and not paying attention, or tolerating harmful behavior or language from someone because, hey, nothing is personal! Actually, the opposite is true. When we can see that nothing is personal, we can divert energy away from thoughts such as *What is wrong with me to cause them to say this?* and shift it to *Do I like how this person makes me feel?*

The greatest result of realizing that nothing is personal is that it frees us from the belief that we're unworthy of love because someone isn't able to give it to us.

The Mirror of Judgment

In the period between my graduating college and my deciding to go back to school to become a therapist, my sense of self felt shaky. I had a marketing job that I knew wasn't fulfilling my purpose, and I was picking up freelance gigs that I knew were short-term fixes for a greater existential question: *What the hell am I supposed to be doing while I'm here on this earth?* Each day at work, this nagging feeling would visit me. So when people asked me, "What do you do for work?" I immediately put my guard up. I took this simple, harmless question as an attack. I heard it as "What are you doing with your life?" because *I* didn't know what I was doing. The question made me face my own discomfort and the uncertainty that I had been trying to push away.

What lingered beneath the defensiveness was a lack of trust in myself, a sense of not having all the answers, and a fear of people noticing this. When I made the decision to go back to school and dedicate my career to supporting people in their healing, that persistent feeling started to recede, and it has continued to disappear as I step into what I now believe is my purpose.

I never actually knew what people were thinking about me. I just created a mean version of other people in my head and used it to torture myself.

Conversely, judging other people can be another way of creating a false sense of control. It temporarily relieves us of the discomfort of our own insecurities. We tend to judge people when they do something outside our own comfort zones, and maybe even for something they do that we wish we also could do. If you believe there are parts of you that must be controlled or shamed, then you'll relate to the external world that way.

NOTHING IS PERMANENT

Things naturally feel less personal when we realize that they're not permanent. Taking something personally simply becomes an uncomfortable thought, with uncomfortable bodily sensations that eventually pass. There's nothing truer about being alive than the impermanent nature of absolutely everything: the intensity of our thoughts, the discomfort of conflict, the mood that we're currently in, the appearance of our bodies. Everything changes. When things aren't going well, it will pass. And when things are going well, it will pass.

Extra suffering comes from (1) clinging or grasping onto some-thing because we don't want it to go away or change or (2) resist-ing or having an aversion to a change because we don't want that change to happen.

When things aren't going well, saying "This will pass" allows us to be present with the pain and discomfort while acknowledging that it will subside. Even when we're in periods of pain that are lasting awhile, we can notice the ways in which that pain is subtly changing and fluctuating.

When things are going well, saying "This will pass" invites us to bask in the sweetness of the moment, appreciating that it won't be that way forever. The mind may then say, *But I don't want this to end! Why does it have to?* We can acknowledge that inner voice as yet another experience that's temporary.

Everything is always changing—how comforting, and how heartbreaking. I feel the comfort of impermanence when I'm se-duced into an anxious thought spiral, or when I'm enduring phys-ical pain, or when I'm feeling stagnant in life, or when a wave of grief washes over me and I suddenly find myself clinging to a ver-sion of reality that's no longer here. *This will pass,* I tell myself, and that reminder allows the pain to move through me and the tears to flow more freely because I know that this fleeting pain isn't my destiny. There's no need to resist it when it's already on its way out.

Acknowledging Death
Invites Us to Live

During my most recent visit with my mom, I found her sleeping, curled into a ball with the blanket pulled over her frail body. Usually when I'd visit, I'd have to search for her: she'd be power walking down the halls of the facility, doing laps around the other residents while muttering to herself, because even though her mind was fading, her body was still quite young. But now her body was declining, too, and the rare sight of her sleeping in her bed made me realize: *We're closer to the end.*

I sat next to her, crying softly, watching her as she rested. After a while she opened her eyes, groggy, and looked up at me. For a split second it felt like she snapped into being Mom again: not Alzheimer's Mom, but *Mom* Mom—the one I had known for the first nineteen years of my life. She stroked my shoulder and said, "Don't worry, Meggy, everything is going to be okay." And then fell back to sleep. I can't explain it, but it felt like a last visit, a last message, from the mom I had been missing.

As my mom has been slowly eaten up by this disease, I've been confronted with what it means to live. Each day at the end of my meditation practice, and sprinkled throughout the day, I spend a few minutes acknowledging to myself that one day I'll die. This practice is called *maranasati*, or mindfulness of death. Bhutan has been shown to be one of the happiest countries on earth, and the Bhutanese culture encourages people to contemplate death five times a day. While meditating on death may sound depressing, I've found it has the opposite effect. In acknowledging death, I'm pulled back into what feels alive right now. I'm reminded of how impermanent life is, and how urgent it is to live. I could die tomorrow. I could die in fifty years. Even if I do everything in my control to prolong my life, I can't know when my breath will be taken from me, and once again I find myself struck by the fragility of this mysterious existence.

I'm simply reminding myself of the truth that everything changes. I used to feel so petrified of death, and I still feel tense around it sometimes, but in accepting it as a fact of life, I'm met with more spaciousness to be with the person who's living and breathing in this physical body, in this earthly realm. It's by acknowledging the impermanence of life that I'm able to meet myself fully. Do I really want to spend my entire life trying to please other people? I'm going to die one day, so I want to live, in a way that feels like living, to *me*.

NOTHING IS PERFECT

Because everything eventually changes, that can only mean that things aren't going to go perfectly, smoothly, or easily all the time.

"Nothing is perfect" means: Of course life is going to suck sometimes. Of course people are sometimes going to be mad at you. Of course you're going to have your heart broken, and get sick, and lose someone or something close to you in this lifetime. Of course. Because that's what it means to be alive, to have a beating heart in this

185

body. Acknowledging that nothing is perfect means being realistic about the nature of being human. This work isn't about not having challenging emotions; it's about changing our relationship to those emotions, not adding an extra layer of suffering on top of them.

Even when we cultivate a greater ability to navigate stress and handle it with more ease, life is still going to have difficulties. "Nothing is perfect" means being honest with ourselves about that reality.

You're Not Perfect: You'll Still Take Some Things Personally

Inevitably, we're going to take things personally. We don't need to be perfect, defenseless beings who are unfazed by anything. The practice of taking things less personally is so hard and imperfect. We can use NICER as a meditation to return to a state of awareness in which we can see things a bit more clearly.

We can **Notice** when we take something personally and see where the mind starts going with it, the stories it starts sucking us into: *They must hate me. I'm the most awkward person on this planet. I should never be allowed to leave the house again.*

We can notice that the mind is going there and **Invite** this scared part of ourselves to stay, saying, *You're allowed to be here,* knowing that fighting those thoughts won't make them go away.

We can then get **C**urious about the story the mind is creating: *What part of me was activated by this story? Is this story even true? Is there actual evidence to back this story up?* Remember: People sometimes *will* be mad at you. People sometimes *will* not like you. We're not lying to ourselves about that inevitable truth but rather soothing ourselves in the midst of discomfort.

We can then **E**mbrace this part of ourselves: *I know this is uncomfortable. You're safe. We're going to move through this together.*

We can then **R**eturn to what's real and true right now as a way to get out of the mind's stories and into the present. Notice your breath, any sounds in the room. Come back to now.

Acceptance ≠ Passivity

There's a common misconception that practicing acceptance means we're being passive. *So if life is imperfect and I accept this moment as it is, does that mean I'll just do nothing? Oh, la dee da, this is life, I guess. If I accept this moment, will I be nothing but a shell of a human who lets life just happen to me?*

No. To practice acceptance of this moment means to see it clearly. It means to see our reality through a clear, grounded lens and say, "This is what's happening. Now what?" We can release our grip on what's not in our control and turn our focus to what we can change. Acceptance means being honest about our reality and saying, "Okay, this is what I'm feeling, and these feelings are allowed to be here. Does something in my world need to change?" It's a balance between leaning back and allowing life to unfold as it's going to and knowing where we can take action.

Release expectations of what this moment "should" look like and instead meet it right now, as it is.

Instead of saying, *I shouldn't be feeling this way!* or *This shouldn't be happening!* we can practice soothing the part of ourselves that's resisting reality and say, *Okay, but this* is *what's happening right now. It won't be this way forever. Now let's see what happens next.*

REFLECTION QUESTIONS

1. What's a comment or judgment that you tend to take quite personally? What part of you is being activated by it?

2. What does this part of you need to feel safe? What feels soothing to this part of you?

It is safe to not be liked
by everyone. I don't
need to control people's
perceptions of me.

CHAPTER

Conflict Is Like Death (It's Inevitable)

How to stop running from discomfort

Arm's Length

"Do you think that keeping people at a distance protects you in a way?" I ask Evelyn.

Evelyn's main reason for coming to therapy was to work through relationship anxiety. She keeps most friends at a safe distance, scared of what could happen if they get too close. She has a big, chunky red scarf wrapped around her neck, and I silently wonder if that's to keep me at a distance, too. Her eyes meet mine for a second before they fall to her lap. She inhales sharply.

"I just feel like I avoid getting too close to people so that we can't get into an argument. If we aren't that close, there can't be any disagreements. And that feels safer. But then it feels terrible when I realize no one really knows me."

As wonderful as it might sound to sit in a cave every waking hour and never have to deal with the possibility of upsetting or disappointing people, that's not real life. There's a Buddhist teaching that describes a student who escaped to a cave to meditate all day. He thought if he could avoid all distractions, he could finally reach enlightenment. For the first couple of days he was serene, meditating from dawn until dusk. But as the days passed, he started to notice a faint *drip drip drip* coming from the back of the cave. And this became his new fixation. He tried to ignore it, but he couldn't, and he grew more and more frustrated, realizing that he had traded one set of distractions for a different one.

Since fawning stems from complex relational trauma (i.e.,

trauma that happens while in relationship to other people), healing happens when we can form relationships that are safe and supportive and reveal the messy parts of ourselves. We heal relational trauma not by *hiding away* from the world but by *being in* the world in a way that feels safe and authentic to us.

So many women, understandably, are petrified of conflict. The greatest irony is that in an attempt to avoid conflict and keep the peace, we create so much more tension within ourselves. When we shove our emotions down—our resentments, our frustrations, our needs—they don't go anywhere, they don't just disappear. When we can accept, or at least acknowledge, that conflict and rupture are inevitable, we can expend so much less energy trying to run from it and more energy working through it.

Running from conflict and hard conversations reinforces the belief that these are things we should be scared of. As we continue to show the scared, protective parts of ourselves that we can have an uncomfortable conversation and still be safe, conflict will start to feel safer. We can't spend our lives running from close relationships, from conflict, because then we're not fully living. Without conflict, we can't grow.

QUICK FACE-YOUR-FEARS CHECKLIST

When conflict arises, try not to panic. Ask yourself these questions:

1. In this moment, is anyone in physical danger?
2. If not, are you avoiding discomfort?
3. If you are safe and avoiding discomfort, ask: *Whose discomfort am I avoiding? Is it someone else's or my own or both?*

4. If you don't address this, how will you likely feel about this situation tomorrow, next week, or in the long term? Will avoiding conflict change how you feel about it in the future?

5. Will avoidance prolong suffering?

Understanding the Root

If you rarely witnessed conflict addressed in a safe and healthy way growing up, you're going to feel scared of it because you think conflict means the relationship is endangered, over, or ruined.

For most of my life, I learned that conflict felt unsafe and had negative consequences, and I believed that having my own opinion meant that I was difficult. So I did the thing that felt smartest and most protective: I avoided conflict at all costs. I didn't know I had a fear of conflict; I thought I just didn't like drama. I would say yes when I wanted to say no, because admitting that I had needs felt too embarrassing or made me seem too needy. I would change my opinion to match what the other person thought so that our conversation wouldn't make them think I disagreed with them. I ignored things that bothered me because I thought addressing something after it had happened would mean that I couldn't let it go and that I was being too sensitive.

What was modeled for me when I was a kid became my default behavior when I became a young adult: *Don't talk about it. Pretend it never happened.* I'd try to move on as quickly as possible: "It's totally

fine!" "OMG, *I'm* sorry!" "No worries!" I didn't know there was another way. I really thought that the truth should be either silenced
or screamed, and that talking about it would 100 percent of the time
lead to feeling more unsafe, to having more love being taken away,
and that didn't feel worth it. I didn't know that facing conflict didn't
have to be a big deal, that it could be a simple acknowledgment.

Learning to Soothe Yourself First

When the mind starts to go *BEEP BEEP BEEP: YOU ARE IN DANGER*
because the other person seems agitated, or you're about to overapologize for something that has nothing to do with you, or you're
about to overexplain yourself because you didn't get the laugh you
were hoping for, then it's time to pause. Slow down. You may still
seek external soothing, and *that is okay!*

The pause is what makes it a win. Your ability to notice the
scared, protective part of you being triggered is a win. There's no
way you can do this healing stuff "wrong."

Mantras to soothe the protective part of you during conflict:

- I'm safe.
- I know this is uncomfortable. We can survive discomfort.
- Conflict can feel scary sometimes, but I'm here with you.
- I'm the parent now and I'll take care of you through this.

- Your needs aren't a burden. It's safe to express your emotions.
- Thank you for trying to protect me. This is a safe situation.

Avoiding Conflict Prevents Connection

Maddy told me about her experience living with a roommate, someone she had met through a friend of a friend. They hit it off right away, watched rom-coms every Thursday night in their pajamas with fistfuls of buttery popcorn, and commuted to work together, since they worked only a block apart. But as each week progressed, Maddy would watch her roommate's dishes pile up in the sink and clothes accumulate on the bathroom floor, and with every plate that was stacked and every shirt that was dropped, Maddy suppressed both her resentment and her desire to ask the roommate to clean up after herself. In the fog of her resentment, she found her annoyance growing, and herself getting frustrated at any and every little thing her roommate did. Their relationship started to become tense, but the tension was never addressed, and they began to drift apart.

"Is everything okay between us? I feel like you've been distant recently," her roommate said to her one day.

"Oh, yeah, I'm totally fine! I've just been so busy."

When Maddy was growing up, her mom's emotions were the center of the family, her reactions so big that they'd fill up whatever room the family was in. Maddy and her brother learned

197

what they had to do—load the dishwasher perfectly; unload it when the dishes were clean; make sure the house was as organized as they could get it—to keep her stress at bay. By needing to prioritize her mom's emotional regulation, Maddy learned two things: (1) how she felt was not a priority, and (2) her emotions stressed people out and caused conflict, which felt scary. Now she avoids conflict at all costs as a way to prevent people from getting upset and because she thinks her emotions aren't worth being acknowledged, that they are "too much," that she's being dramatic when she feels them.

"I thought talking about what was bothering me with my roommate would be the meanest thing I could ever do," Maddy says to me with a laugh.

"So what ended up happening?" I ask.

"Oh, I never brought it up. When our lease was almost over, I just sent her an apologetic text with a random excuse about why I was going to live somewhere else."

"What were you scared of?"

"I was scared of how she'd react, if she would get upset with me and then we wouldn't be able to recover from it. The irony isn't lost on me, by the way, that we ended up losing touch because I didn't talk about things," she says.

Becoming aware of the unconscious way you handle conflict is the first step in changing your relationship to it.

When we're in a fawn response, the fearful part of us chooses dishonest harmony over deep, authentic connection. Real connection requires letting ourselves be seen and sometimes giving or receiving feedback that's hard to hear. Honest, clear, and open communication is the most important part of any close and safe relationship, whether it's with a family member, a romantic partner, a friend, or a coworker. But both people need to be willing to participate. If one person is wanting and willing to have open communication and the other person dodges topics that need to be addressed, the closeness can go only so far.

Admitting that there is something you don't see eye to eye on means confronting the fear that the other person will leave or think of you differently. When we can practice tolerating the discomfort of our emotions and remembering that external events are not reflections of our worth, lovability, or inherent goodness, conflict becomes less scary. It no longer means something bigger and deeper than it is.

Procrastination Is an Emotional Mind Game

Anytime I'm working with a client on procrastination, the question I ask is: "What uncomfortable emotion are you avoiding?" Procrastination is rarely about the task itself (you know you're physically capable of sending an email, for example); it's about avoiding the uncomfortable questions that arise when doing the task: *Am I good enough? Am I a phony? Do they think I'm stupid?*

Avoiding the task makes us feel in control of those emotions. Imagine sitting at your computer, trying to get a task done. Suddenly, you find yourself picking up your phone to scroll. In that split second, some uncomfortable emotion has been triggered—*This task is hard, I don't want to do this*—and the mind says, *I don't want to feel this! How can I get rid of it?* So you grab your phone and scroll without consciously thinking about it. You're doing this to avoid some sort of uncomfortable emotion. I know. The mind is so sneaky, and conflict avoidance is no different.

Just Do It

Let's practice getting comfortable with the discomfort of:

- Saying "Thank you" in response to someone's apology instead of "No worries! It's totally fine!"
- Acknowledging conflict after the fact as a way to communicate to the other person "Your feelings and needs matter to me."
- Allowing yourself to revisit a conversation that has "passed" because it keeps coming up internally. Taking accountability for your mistakes even if that means admitting you're not perfect.
- Saying "Thank you for sharing that with me—I'm listening and I want to understand" instead of getting defensive.
- Releasing the idea that someone has to be "right" and someone has to be "wrong" when people are having a hard conversation.

It's Not Your Job to Manage Their Discomfort

Over the past few months, Miranda has noticed that she keeps getting interrupted by her colleague during their brainstorming sessions. She'll be in the middle of a thought and see an idea churning in his head, and the excitement takes over. He'll blurt out his idea, and her thought gets shut down. There's never any acknowledgment that he interrupted her, and he doesn't circle back to her to say, "Miranda, I'm sorry I interrupted you. What were you saying before?" This happens again and again. She has a solid relationship with this colleague and doesn't think he's interrupting her and sidelining her ideas knowingly or maliciously, but she's still nervous about bringing it up.

"What if he just shuts down? What if he gets defensive?" she asks me.

"All you can control is what you say and how you say it. You can't control how he receives it," I remind her.

Miranda realizes that her energy has been spent trying to prevent her colleague's discomfort, to not make him feel bad, but in exchange for avoiding those risks, she's left feeling silenced every week. What Miranda wants, she realizes, is simply to point out what she's been noticing and how it's making her feel. She decides to focus less on her colleague's reaction and more on what she wants to say, which is something like, "I've noticed that sometimes when I'm speaking in meetings, I get interrupted. I know that you may not realize you're doing it; I'm wondering if you can be mindful of it so that I can finish my thought." Whether he receives these comments well or gets defensive, Miranda will have been successful in communicating what was on her mind.

When we practice clear, direct, open, and honest communication, the other person is going to respond or react in their own way, dependent on their ability to handle discomfort. All we can ever control is our own words and actions and how we respond to other people. As you practice communicating more clearly, it's not your job to manage other people's discomfort.

By accepting that conflict is inevitable, we're also accepting:

- **The fact that someone's in a bad mood doesn't automatically mean it's your fault or your responsibility to "fix" it (unless you've harmed someone, of course).** What you *can* do is offer them support and space to emotionally regulate themself.
- **You can support someone in their emotional experience without *becoming* their emotional experience.** You can be there for them while also being aware of what's happening in your body and what you're needing. In fact, by being aware of what's happening to you, you can support them more authentically and sustainably.
- **Sometimes people *will* be mad at you, or disagree with you, or not understand you.** When you can accept that these things will happen, your energy moves away from trying so hard to prevent them and controlling how others work through their emotions.

Being a clear, direct communicator is a practice of self-trust, a balance between knowing when to bring something up because it needs to be addressed and knowing when to surrender control and lean back in the relationship. Bringing something up doesn't come from a place of control; it comes from a place of connection. The more we try to manage or control someone else's behavior, the more suffering we're creating for ourselves.

Take Their Word for It

"Are you *sure* you're not mad at me?" Ilana asked her sister. They had just gotten into a minor argument, and as the tension began to ease, Ilana started to get into her own head. Her sister's default demeanor was cool, calm, and collected, and sometimes her neutrality activated anxiety for Ilana. The succinct communication left extra space for her to overthink: *What if she's secretly upset and just isn't telling me? That's what Mom does.*

"I'm not mad at you, Ilana. But I *am* starting to get annoyed at you because of how much you're asking me if I'm mad at you," her sister replied.

If you avoid conflict, you may unconsciously believe that others are avoiding it, too. You may assume that they're secretly mad and just not bringing it up *because that's how you handle conflict.*

One of the most important and challenging practices I want you to take away from this book is this: Take their word for it. Get comfortable with the discomfort of taking what people say at face value without imagining what else it could mean or what they could secretly be feeling.

If someone is being passive-aggressive in their communication and not bringing something to you directly, there's nothing for you to fix.

The other week, Ilana was on the phone with her mom when her mom suddenly started being short, responding to Ilana's questions with "mm-hmms" and heavy sighs. "I'm *fine*, Ilana," her mom said after Ilana asked if everything was okay. At thirty-two, Ilana knew her mom well enough to sense that she wasn't fine, that she was upset about something but wouldn't say it directly. Normally, Ilana would try to butter her mom up, such as by orchestrating weekend plans that Ilana really wasn't interested in or telling her about a work accomplishment to shift the mood. Instead, Ilana said, "Okay. I trust that you'll tell me if something's bothering you, and I'll be here to listen."

When someone is being a passive-aggressive communicator, the protective part of us will try to jump in and fawn, because the discomfort of not knowing what the other person is thinking or feeling can be intolerable. Yet all you can do is offer the other person space and support.

Flip the script: the same is true for you. Because you learned the niche skill of picking up on other people's needs and emotions without them saying anything, you may unconsciously expect that others can do that, too. You may expect other people to just know what you're feeling and what you're thinking, and you may be upset because you have the ability to do that. They can't read your mind—and it's no longer your job to read theirs. Nor should you or anyone else have to work so hard to master ESP.

Avoiding Conflict Versus Drama

I've always preferred close, one-on-one relationships to having big groups of friends. When I was growing up, I'd tell myself that I just didn't like the potential drama of big groups, but I think beneath that statement was fear. The more friends I had, the more people I could upset and disappoint. Too many reactions to manage, too many faces to scan, too many emotions to monitor, too much potential for conflict, and it just felt less exhausting to focus on one relationship at a time, one face at a time. Now, as an adult, my preference is the same—to have closer, more intimate one-on-one relationships—but my reason for that feels different in my body. It no longer comes from a place of fear and avoidance. I'd rather keep my circle small and tight-knit so that I can give the dear people in it more of me and still have enough left for myself.

While growing up, Amy would watch her parents bicker like she was watching a Ping-Pong match, her head snapping left and right, trying to keep score. She'd insert herself to mediate the situation, become the voice of reason, the external witness who could point out what was happening. Her parents relied on her outside perspective, each pleading for her to take their side.

Now, as an adult, she goes home for Thanksgiving and watches the same dynamic play out, but this time she leans back, thinking, *This isn't conflict that I need to be a part of. This is drama that I can just observe and stay out of.*

With fawning, our safety comes from making sure that everyone else is happy. We sense conflict, and our instinct is to extinguish it because we learned that we can't feel safe until it's gone. As we heal the fawn response, we see that not all conflict is worth getting wrapped up in—that sometimes there's nothing for us to do.

Accepting that conflict is inevitable—that *it's going to happen*—means that not every point of conflict has to be a huge deal. Sometimes we're just hungry. Or tired. Or overstimulated because the TV was too loud and our partner was trying to talk over it. There's a difference between avoiding conflict (fear-based) and avoiding drama (healthy). It's seeing the difference between *Is this worth bringing up? Can I let this go because it's something that I need to just accept about this person?* and *Is this a repeating pattern that comes up again and again and gets shoved aside as a form of avoidance? Is this someone I even want to have a relationship with? Am I trying to change someone who has shown me again and again that they won't change?*

Resolving conflict becomes far more important in relationships that we're committed to having in our lives.

Avoiding conflict comes from a place of fear.

Staying out of unnecessary drama comes from a place of ease and confidence.

Direct communication *supports* drama-free relationships because it cuts through assumptions. It erases the need to read minds, play games, or read between the lines.

Secondhand Fawning

"I have this really niche pet peeve—if a friend of mine or my partner is doing something that I wouldn't do, I get really anxious and try to control the situation," Hannah explains. When I ask for an example, she says, "Like if my partner is texting a mutual friend of ours in a way I wouldn't, like it isn't people-pleasey enough, I'll get anxious that the recipient is going to receive it the wrong way . . . and it'll reflect badly on me. So I'll try to control what my partner says. Does that make sense?"

"Absolutely. And what do you fear will happen?" I ask.

Hannah looks off, considering. "That people will think of my partner—and therefore me because I'm associated with them—as bad . . . and that we'll get in trouble or they'll be mad, I guess."

I nod, remembering how just last week I noticed my body fully tense up when a few of my friends were laughing and chatting (as people do) at a completely normal, appropriate volume as they came up the stairs to my apartment. I felt a wave of anxiety wash over me, fearful that my neighbors would be annoyed and that I'd get in trouble. I took a deep breath. I knew that this was a younger part of me that had needed to tiptoe around her home to feel safe. I said to that fear, *This is okay. There's no danger here.*

With the fawn response, so much of conflict prevention is an attempt to control the narrative and to deter someone from possibly thinking you're anything other than good. When something feels out of control in our environment—when we notice someone not fawning in a situation in which we would fawn—the protective part of our brain kicks into gear and tries to control anything or anyone in the environment that feels, to the body, like a threat.

I call this *secondhand fawning*, when we're fawning on someone else's behalf, when we're trying to get someone else to fawn because that's what we'd do in the situation. Because we're associated with that person, we attempt to appease others through their behavior and actions as a way to feel safe.

While Victoria was growing up, her dad was highly critical of external things like her appearance and social etiquette. Dinner each night felt like a formal interview. A simple question like, "How was your day?" had to be answered strongly and clearly, and if her dad wasn't satisfied with her answer or delivery, he'd berate her. "You're not going to make it in the real world with *that* answer," he'd say.

Now Victoria is in her fifties, in a long-term relationship with her partner, Bill, who's reserved and soft-spoken. They're on speakerphone with her dad, and Bill's catching him up on his family in a hushed tone. Victoria starts to feel agitated, her body remembering what would happen if her dad wasn't hearing a loud and proud delivery. Victoria starts to nudge Bill. "Speak up," she mouths to him. Confused, Bill keeps speaking in his soft voice. Victoria resorts to hand signals, pointing her thumb up to say, *TALK LOUDER*. She starts to tense up, holding her breath in anticipation of her dad's critical feedback.

In this moment, Victoria's younger self has come to the foreground and is trying to make her partner conform to the communication style that historically granted Victoria safety with her dad. She is fawning—through Bill.

This pattern recently came up with my client George. A few years ago, George went no-contact with his uncle after enduring years of emotional abuse from him. His uncle's birthday was coming up, and George's mom kept pressuring George to give his uncle a call, wish him a happy birthday, and forgive him.

"Why do you want me to do that?" George asked his mom. "You know our history."

"I just think if you don't, he'll be upset," his mom replied.

This was a classic fawning situation—appeasing the abuser to feel safe in the abuser's presence—and George's mom was secondhand fawning—fawning through George—out of fear that it would reflect poorly on her if George didn't reach out. George explained to his mom that this was his boundary, which he wanted to maintain, and that it wasn't his job to manage his uncle's discomfort— or his mom's reaction to his boundary.

The Art of Repair

There's no such thing as a perfect parent, child, partner, or friend. Let that be a relief. You don't need to be perfect in relationships. And when we can stop expecting perfection from ourselves in relationships, we can stop expecting it from others. We're all going to mess up, say things we didn't mean, misunderstand each other's needs, miscommunicate our wants. How we *repair* those moments is what makes relationships even closer.

Let's be clear: I am not talking about relationships that are abusive or conflict that happens again and again in a harmful, cyclical pattern. As you'll read, two crucial components of repair are an active effort to understand the other person's needs and an aim to better self-regulate in the future. Understanding that rupture is inevitable in a relationship doesn't mean that we need to tolerate toxic cycles of conflict when there's little or no effort to reflect and grow coming from the other person. We can have compassion for someone's pain and unprocessed trauma while also protecting ourselves. We can understand why someone is acting the way they are while not excusing or tolerating their behavior.

True repair requires the other person to want to repair, too.

TO REPAIR MEANS TO:

1. Go back to the moment of tension or disconnection and acknowledge what happened.
2. Take responsibility.

3. Share what you learned from the rupture and what you're practicing for next time.

Fawners are rarely taught how to repair. How can something be learned if it wasn't modeled? How can it be taught if our care-givers didn't know how to do it themselves? As kids, so many of us heard "Say you're sorry!" as a way to repair a rupture, but what carries meaning is not the forced, muttered "Sorry" but the inten-tion behind it. A simple apology can actually close off an opportu-nity for conversation. It says, "Here! Take my apology! Are we good now?" Which translates to "Can you get over it already?" Repair, on the other hand, opens up an opportunity for conversation and connection. It's an invitation to understand each other.

We learned in chapter 1 about how self-blame becomes a cop-ing mechanism in high-tension or high-conflict households. When a parent goes from being safe to being scary, or silent, or emotionally absent, the child yearns to find a sense of safety again, to return to a feeling that everything is okay. When there's no repair from the par-ent, when the child is left to make sense of it on their own, they use self-blame as an adaptive coping mechanism. It feels soothing for them to believe *Something is wrong with me. I'm bad. I'm unlovable*, because then they can hold on to the belief that their parents, and the world around them, are safe. If something's wrong with the child, then the problem isn't that the parents can't meet the child's needs.

Without repair, we learned that we were personally responsible for other people's reactions and behaviors. We learned that when

ff22

someone is upset, it was because we did something to make them feel that way.

Repair rewrites those stories.

When we can face conflict and practice repairing it with the other person and with ourselves, we create a new ending to the story, we learn a new lesson from it, and we begin to create new associations with conflict. We show that scared, protective part of ourselves that conflict can lead to more closeness.

Repair also includes repairing with ourselves—separating our behavior from our sense of self. We can say, "I yelled, and I'm not proud of that—I want to work on regulating my emotions," while *also* saying, "This moment in time is not who I am as a person." Repair doesn't excuse our behavior; it allows us to reflect on how we want to behave differently next time.

So much of what we're craving from relationships is a simple acknowledgment that the other person is seeing what we're seeing. When I work with an adult who has or had strained relationships with their parents, whether they are twenty-three or fifty-three, the common thread I hear is deep longing for acknowledgment from the parent that what they're feeling is real and seen. At any age, how healing would it be to hear from a parent, "Hey, I've been reflecting on your childhood and I'm realizing that there were a lot of times I hurt you. And I know I can't change the past, but I'm sorry for the ways I didn't show up for you and I'm working on being a more present parent now"? This simple acknowledgment doesn't wipe away the pain, but it's an opportunity to be seen and heard in a way that wasn't happening before.

When we feel something unsaid lingering in the air, sometimes acknowledgment is all we're craving. Think of any sort of rupture in a relationship, then, as an opportunity for more closeness.

Whether it's with your child, your friend, or your coworker—on the other side of a rupture in the relationship is an opportunity to know each other better, to understand each other's needs more intimately. Again, I'm speaking here about relationships that are healthy. The relationships that feel meaningful and safe to you, in which the other person is willing to listen and be open to mending the rupture together.

Do You Still Love Me? Reassurance Versus Validation

I once worked with Sam and Alicia, a couple who had been together for two years. Sam was a more avoidant type, and Alicia was a more anxious type (a really common pairing, by the way). Because Sam was more avoidant, he'd find himself pulling away during conflict and craving space, which triggered Alicia's anxiety even more: she feared that he was going to leave or that the relationship was ruined forever.

In moments of anxiety, Alicia would seek reassurance as an unconscious way to feel safe again, to know that everything was okay, which usually sounded like "Are you mad at me? Did I do something wrong? Do you still love me?" Conflict triggered Alicia's abandonment wound. She grew up in a home where conflict meant that she had done something wrong, she would get blamed and would be left alone to make sense of it. That's the thing about abandonment: whether it's physical or emotional, it feels the same to the body. So Alicia learned that someone being in a bad mood = *I'm alone, and that feels horrible.*

Of course Sam, who's more avoidant, craves being alone when he's in conflict. Yet he would express that need in a way that felt neglectful and dismissive to Alicia, further activating her anxiety. Alicia felt hurt. Sam shut down. And the cycle continued.

What was necessary for successful repair in their relationship was their first sharing what was going on internally for both of them and then understanding the ways in which each of them had witnessed conflict growing up and what conflict meant to them. For Alicia, the reaction was closeness. For Sam, it was distance. And both of their reactions made sense. Alicia wanted closeness not because she was trying to smother Sam but because she was scared. Sam wanted space not because he was leaving Alicia but because his system had learned to be alone in conflict and to take space. *How* they were communicating those needs mattered.

Another important component of repair—and of soothing the fawn response in general—is knowing the difference between reassurance and validation.

Seeking reassurance means asking the other person to extinguish your fear. "No, I'm not mad at you! Everything is fine!" *Phew.* It provides fleeting relief, but it doesn't address or acknowledge the challenging emotions. Reassurance seeking comes from a habitual, compulsive place, where you feel almost as if you're vomiting words and questions out of urgency, such as repeatedly asking if your partner still loves you or if everything is okay. It happens when we're no longer in our bodies but swirling in our heads. Because reassurance is only temporarily satisfying, it can create a dependency cycle in which a person asks for reassurance again and again, every time the initial relief wears off. Reassurance is one-sided; the anxious person urgently asks the other person to put out the anxiety fire.

Alicia would seek endless reassurance in moments of conflict as a way to soothe the part of herself that felt scared of being abandoned: *If he tells me he loves me, I won't feel anxious anymore.* But reassurance was just a bandage on her gaping abandonment wound. Because she wasn't acknowledging the anxiety itself, her craving for reassurance continued. No amount of reassurance would heal the deeper wound.

Receiving validation is having your feelings and experiences acknowledged and getting confirmation that what you're feeling is legitimate. It's integral to repair. Unlike looking for reassurance, which is to alleviate anxiety, the goal of seeking validation is to be heard, to feel understood and accepted, and to know that your emotions are recognized.

It's pausing and being attuned to what you're feeling and then expressing it in a grounded way.

Validation might include some reassurance ("I'm not mad at you"), but it's also slowing down and communicating to the other person that you hear the emotion beneath their worry ("I can hear that you're feeling anxious. I want to understand what's going on"). Validation doesn't necessarily alleviate the concern, but it says to the other person, "I hear you, your feelings are valid, and I want to understand." Validation comes from connection, presence, and mutual engagement.

Very often, when someone comes to us with something that's emotionally hard, our instinct is to jump into advice giving as a way to alleviate their pain. But this communicates to the other person "Your emotions are too much for me" when they just want their feelings to be heard and acknowledged.

Excessive reassurance seeking can really put a strain on relationships because of its repetitive nature and the burden and pressure it places on others. On the flip side, pausing and letting someone in on what's happening emotionally for you can strengthen a relationship by letting the other person into your inner experience and making them aware of your deepest needs.

In Sam and Alicia's relationship, what was ultimately soothing for Alicia was to learn to understand what emotion was behind the need to ask for reassurance. If she paused and acknowledged that emotion within herself, practiced soothing herself, and communicated that emotion to Sam, Alicia could understand what he was needing.

For Alicia, self-soothing was taking deep breaths or going for a walk and telling herself, *This is anxiety. Okay, this is allowed to be here. I'm safe.*

For Sam, instead of abruptly leaving the room and giving Alicia the silent treatment, self-soothing meant saying something like, "I'm feeling overwhelmed right now and I can feel this conversation escalating. I'm going to take a walk. Let's talk about this more in an hour. I love you and I'm not going anywhere; I just need some time to myself."

This was helpful for both of them because it gave Alicia the soothing she needed, which allowed her to self-regulate, and that allowed Sam to get the space he needed because he wasn't being asked to reassure Alicia again and again. They went from opponents to teammates.

For many of us, the need for reassurance, or even validation, can feel insatiable because we've learned to block any nourishment or care, even if it's what we're wanting and asking for. We've learned to be cautious about taking it in. If in our childhoods love and nourishment were given and then withheld, we learned that it was better to not accept them at all so we could prevent disappointment.

Or maybe it was impossible to receive nourishment without also receiving something that didn't feel good, like being guilt-tripped or controlled. For example, we might have had a caregiver who gave us emotional support only when they were overbearing, or we might have been able to receive care only when we were also being criticized. If in our early experiences taking in nourishment from someone else came with a price, we're going to resist it or not fully absorb it, so no amount of reassurance or validation will feel like enough. We'll always be starving for more.

True, long-term safety arises internally through validating our own emotions, soothing ourselves, and allowing ourselves to receive validation from someone else.

Before You Ask, "Are You Mad at Me?"

When we *react*, there's no pause between the trigger and what we say or do. Our reactions are instant and they're driven by our fears, beliefs, biases, and past experiences.

If there's a perceived distance in a relationship and it activates the part of you that fears that the other person is upset with you, ask yourself these questions:

- Is the story I'm telling myself absolutely true?
- Is this different from the other person's usual behavior, or is it consistent with how they communicate?
- Could there be other reasons for the other person's perceived distance (their work is stressful, they're overwhelmed, they're in the honeymoon stage of a new romantic relationship, they're going through a breakup)?
- Are you expecting this person to be a version of themselves that they no longer are? Are you clinging to a past version of the relationship?
- Does something need to be addressed within the relationship?

The Worst-Case Scenario Is Clarity

"If I stopped reaching out to this person, I genuinely think we'd never talk again."

Amelia noticed herself feeling resentment when she realized that she was the only one maintaining a long-distance friendship. With each week or month that went by, she found this resentment growing.

"Do you think you want to share your feelings with her?" I asked her during one session.

"I do, yeah. I'm scared, but I think I need to tell her how I'm feeling and understand what's going on with her."

The next time they chatted, Amelia took a deep breath and nervously asked her friend, "Do you mind if I talk to you about something? I've been feeling that you're distant recently, and I wanted to check in and see if everything is okay."

In that conversation, her friend said that she'd just been super-busy and hadn't had the time to keep up with people the way she used to. Amelia listened to her while also holding her hurt, because she knew that her friend was making time for other friends but wasn't putting in the effort with her. More weeks went by, the friend still wasn't reaching out, and the pattern continued.

But now it felt different for Amelia because she had clarity on what the friend was able to give to her. Amelia's energy shifted away from trying to get her friend to change and toward accepting that this was what she was going to get from this friend. This allowed Amelia to lean back a little more in the relationship, to loosen her grip on what she wanted it to be. Taking it a step further, she realized that this friendship was mirroring her relationship with her dad, in which she had learned that in order for her to feel loved in a relationship, she needed to work really hard. That uncomfortable conversation with her friend made clear to Amelia that she shouldn't have to bend over backward to convince someone to care. Nothing much changed in the relationship, but Amelia was able to surrender more within it.

The worst-case scenario is clarity. Or rather, more realistically, it's discomfort and clarity. Yes, it's hard to have certain conversations and to look at the reality of the relationship that's right in front of you, but when you do, *then you know*, and you can use your precious energy to accept what's happening, accept that you can't control the other person or change them, and move forward. Then you're closer to the truth and have the information you need to make the next best decision.

The discomfort of having direct conversations is temporary, but resentment festers and keeps us stuck in endless conflict with ourselves.

Set Yourself Free

When you're trying to decide whether it's even worth it to have an uncomfortable conversation—like with a parent who won't hear you or an ex who's stuck in their defensiveness—shift the focus to have it be for you.

Regardless of whether the other person hears or understands you, regardless of how they react or respond, the success of the conversation is solely based on you communicating what is on your mind. Many times, clients find that telling the other person what's going on for them dissolves the need to have the conversation because they realize, *Oh, I just wanted to have this conversation to see if the other person would change. Now I know I'm trying to be heard by someone who won't hear me.*

When the conversation is just for you and your desire to express what you're feeling, you may decide it's not worth having and record a voice memo of what you want to say, or write a letter you don't send.

Even if you don't have the uncomfortable conversation, at the very least you can acknowledge to yourself the anger, the resentment, the betrayal that you feel. If the other person won't validate your emotions, give yourself the gift of validating yourself.

DO YOU HAVE A SEC? CHEAT SHEET FOR FACING CONFLICT: THE FOUR WHATS

When you're trying to decide if you should bring something up, pause and ask yourself these questions:

1. WHAT AM I FEELING RIGHT NOW? Angry? Unheard? Frustrated?

2. WHAT IS MY INTENTION IN BRINGING THIS UP? Do I just want to be heard, or am I hoping for something from the other person, like a response or change? There's no right or wrong here—it's just helpful to understand what you're expecting.

3. WHAT DO I WANT TO SAY TO THIS PERSON? Communicate from a place of "I." Resist the urge to speak for them or to make black-and-white statements such as "You're always so . . ."

4. WHAT DO I NEED FROM THIS PERSON AND/OR MYSELF? What, if anything, are you asking from the other person? If they don't give you the response you're looking for, what will you need to be okay? If they don't give you the validation you're craving, can you give it to yourself?

This is uncomfortable work, but on the other side of it is a greater ability to speak honestly and clearly, healthier relationships, clarity about whom you want to spend your time with, and more energy because you're no longer wasting energy by dodging conflict left and right. Conflict is like death: it's inevitable.

REFLECTION QUESTIONS

1. What's your current relationship to conflict?

2. When there's a perceived conflict, what do you fear will happen if you face it?

3. What do you need during conflict, whether it's from yourself or the other person, that would feel soothing to you?

Conflict is a natural part of life. I am capable of tolerating the discomfort of conflict.

CHAPTER

Rebranding Boundaries

The freedom of honoring your needs

Eternal Summer

When my husband and I moved to California, I found myself grieving winter. I do miss snow, the oddly nice feeling of losing sensation in my fingers and toes, and the nostalgic smell of wet mittens, but it turns out what I had really cherished about winter was the collective, seasonal permission to rest. I had relied on winter to give me an easy excuse to stay home, to cancel plans, to not overextend myself, to do less. Winter gave me the space that I couldn't freely give to myself.

I forced my body to be in an eternal state of summer when it didn't need to be: doing high-intensity workouts every single day with no rest in between; stuffing every second of my weekend with plans because sitting still was too uncomfortable; mindlessly opening up my email when the workday was done because "turning off" was alarming to the part of me that felt valuable only when I was achieving and doing something productive.

My inability to say no was rooted in not wanting to be left behind, not wanting to be abandoned. *If I say yes, I can't disappoint anyone. If I say yes, I won't "fall behind" in my closeness to this person, and I'll still be relevant to them, and then maybe they won't forget about me. If I neglect myself, maybe I won't be neglected by them.* When I began to realize that this was my automatic process, I noticed that my immediate thought was usually, *I should say yes*, and I began to replace that thought with a more conscious inquiry: *Do I have to say yes?* And if the answer was *No, it's not obligatory*, the question shifted to: *Do I want to?* Oftentimes the answer is still yes, but the difference lies in the process of getting there. I no longer say yes for fear of abandonment by others; I say yes because I'm not willing to abandon myself.

While stuck in the fawn response, I feared that setting boundaries meant I would be harsh, closed off, selfish. By honoring my needs and setting boundaries, I now do so much more for the people I love, and it comes from a genuine place. I have more capacity to show up for the people who feel like chosen family to me, and I want to show up for them because I have the energy to give. And when I don't have the energy to give, I trust myself to get the rest and recovery that I need to replenish myself.

Redefining Boundaries

Boundaries need a rebrand. They're usually described as robotic and stiff, often paired with cold, corporate-lingo scripts. The boundaries you set don't need to conform to other people's boundaries—they just have to feel authentic to *you*.

A boundary means knowing ourselves and our needs. Every healthy relationship has some sort of boundary, because in a healthy relationship, each person is able to be themselves.

Imagine that you have dinner plans with your best friend tonight. You're blankly standing in front of your closet, deciding whether you can endure wearing pants with a zipper for the duration of the evening, when you hear your phone *ding*. You reach for it, and there's a text from your friend: she's canceling. Let's pause the video here.

What would you rather have your friend do?

1. **LIE.** You might feel suspicious, but you aren't going to accuse her of making up an excuse. You might ruminate on whether she's replacing you with that new, superfun friend she made last month in her pottery class.
   Or

2. **SHARE HOW SHE'S FEELING.** "Hey, I was really looking forward to our dinner tonight. But, honestly, I'm exhausted and I don't think I'm up for it right now. I just need to marinate in my bathtub. Is it okay if we reschedule?"

I have to imagine that you'd prefer the latter. Maybe you'd even be touched that your friend trusted you enough to tell you the truth. Maybe her telling you the truth would give you permission to be honest with her about how you were feeling the next time you just wanted to veg on the couch. Not only would you *not* be mad at your friend for telling you the truth but you would respect her. True intimacy means never having to wonder if someone is mad at you, because the standard for the relationship is honesty. Having boundaries doesn't mean turning into a flaky, unreliable friend. It's striking a balance between showing up for the people you want in your life and for yourself.

Boundaries are bridges, not walls, and they create space for sustainable connections to thrive. Boundaries aren't attempts to change the other person but ways to feel rooted in yourself while being in relationship to others. Consider these questions about any of your relationships, whether they feel safe or unstable: If you were to accept that the other person would never change, what relationship would you want to have with them? What would you need in the relationship in order for you to feel okay?

Boundaries Come in Many Flavors

- Time
- Financial
- Energetic
- Physical/body
- Sexual
- Intellectual
- Spiritual/religious
- Material (belongings)

Boundaryless

As a child, Alex rarely witnessed her parents setting boundaries— with work, their friends, or their community. She'd watch as her mom rolled her eyes at the caller ID and then picked up the phone with a chirpy, "Mary! I was just thinking about you!" Alex's dad was a leader at their church, so it felt like the family's duty to say yes to everything and support everyone else without ever thinking

ARE YOU MAD AT ME?

about first supporting themselves. She witnessed her parents grow tired and resentful but also saw how they took a certain pride in what they were doing: giving and giving and giving, and being *seen* giving, even if this endless effort drained their emotional energy.

Alex learned that not having boundaries made you good, that if you weren't suffering from overextension, you weren't doing enough, and there were consequences for that. Yet she watched as her parents got burned out and grew bitter, and they seemed to lose more of their enjoyment of serving others the more they pushed themselves past their capacity.

As an adult, Alex experiences the wrath of insurmountable guilt anytime she sets a boundary with someone, feeling like she's a bad friend, partner, or daughter if she has needs in the first place, let alone expresses them.

So many of us who are stuck in the fawn response never learned the value of boundaries because, as we were growing up, there was no distinction between our outer and inner worlds. Fawners don't know how to set boundaries because we learned that in order to receive love, we have to do *more*, give *more*. So we say yes to everything. When we are adults, this means overextending ourselves; feeling resentful; not knowing who we are and what we need, like, and prefer; and neglecting ourselves over the long term for the short-term safety of pleasing someone else.

In order for us to be able to set boundaries, we first have to know what our needs are. We have to reconnect with questions such as *What do I feel? What do I want? What do I need?*

Nice Versus Compassionate

"I can't say no. I'm just too nice of a person," Carter explains, and then she talks about how annoying it is that her friend asked Carter to look after her dog while the friend is out of town—for the fourth weekend in a row.

"Can I challenge you on that for a sec? If you're saying yes but secretly bubbling with resentment, is that actually being nice?"

For fawners, people who often fear being seen as bad, healing the fawn response feels like dangerous territory. "So does that mean I'm going to be . . . *mean*?" (and therefore, be *seen* as mean, and therefore bad). No, it doesn't mean that you're going to transform into an asshole at the stroke of midnight. **Healing the fawn response means focusing less on being nice and more on being compassionate.** And being compassionate doesn't mean always being "nice."

In Compassion-Focused Therapy, derived from Buddhism, "compassion" is defined as "a sensitivity to suffering of self and others, with a commitment to try to alleviate it and prevent it."[1] It's about alleviating long-term suffering, which may require facing uncomfortable situations in the short term. Niceness is about how you're being perceived—it's doing something for the sake of being seen as good. Compassion isn't about being liked; it's about being connected to ourselves, because we can't be compassionate to others if we're not also being compassionate to ourselves. We're not being compassionate if we're abandoning ourselves in the process.

We tend to fawn as a way to avoid our own discomfort and manage other people's emotions, but that behavior actually creates more long-term suffering within ourselves and in the relationship. Out of unspoken resentment, maybe we're telling lots of white lies to avoid setting clear boundaries, but white lies create so much more tension and unhappiness within us. Clear, direct communication reduces long-term suffering, even if it brings about short-term discomfort, because it cuts through and addresses the situation that's right in front of us. If our efforts to make everyone else happy are making us really unhappy, we're not on a sustainable path.

Ask yourself: *Do I really mean what I'm about to say? Am I saying something I don't mean to try to appease the other person?*

Boundaries acknowledge our anger and resentment in a productive way, redirecting these challenging emotions that usually go inward and putting them toward something that's supportive.

Compassion can mean saying no, being firm, being fierce, being honest.

True Empathy Requires Boundaries

When we're tapped into ourselves, when we're grounded in our bodies, we have a deeper ability to be empathetic, because our brains aren't hyperfocused on trying to stay safe. In healing the fawn response, we're strengthening our ability to discern: *Is this emotion mine? Or am I holding it for someone else?*

With the fawn response, we're feeling other people's emotions while completely giving up our sense of self. Fawning enmeshes us with our environment, with the people around us: suddenly their anger becomes our anger, and their anxiety becomes our anxiety. Healing the fawn response means remaining grounded and steady in your inner experience so that you can distinguish between what's your responsibility and what's out of your control.

A Crisis Will Test Our Boundaries

Stacy's phone buzzes on her nightstand. She groggily reaches for it, squinting at the bright screen: Ethan—her younger brother. Her heart drops, and her mind travels to any worst-case scenario she can conjure up.

"Ethan?"

"Stacy, I need your help," he says, his voice trembling. "I lost my job last month and now I can't make rent. They're going to evict me if I don't pay by tomorrow."

"Why are you telling me this *now*?" she says, looking at her clock: it's 3:30 a.m. "Never mind. How much do you need?"

She wires him the money, wincing as she watches it leave her bank account. She gets by on her own but doesn't have a lot of extra money floating around.

"Thank you, Stacy. I promise I'll pay you back," he says. She knows he won't (he never does) but she thanks him anyway.

In our session now, she describes having spent the rest of the night wide-awake in bed, worrying about Ethan and worrying about herself if he keeps asking for more money.

When we're in a crisis, whether it's our own or we're supporting someone else through theirs, we probably won't have time to pause, look inward, and assess our needs. That makes sense: our body is focused on squelching the crisis in front of us. Crises naturally disconnect us from ourselves because they send us into necessary survival mode. You might slip into a fawn response during a crisis even with people whom you've stopped doing that with in normal, day-to-day life. Once the crisis passes, you can return to yourself, process what happened, and give your emotions and needs the space they couldn't get in the moment.

In the aftermath of the crisis, Stacy felt a medley of emotions. She felt angry that Ethan hadn't asked for help sooner. She felt resentful that no one else in her family had picked up his call. Then she felt guilty for feeling anger and resentment. She wanted to help her brother, of course, but she also needed to take care of herself. She knew that showing up for her brother long-term meant getting clear with herself on what she was able to give him. She knew that if she kept giving and giving with no boundaries, she'd hit a breaking point and have no empathy left.

The questions we considered in our session were: *How much am I willing and able to give before it gets to a point of resentment? How can I support him while also taking care of myself? What boundaries do I need with him and myself in future moments of crisis?*

Now that the crisis had passed, Stacy needed to calm the panicked part of herself that felt compelled to rescue her brother. It meant tuning in to what she was feeling and needing and being honest with herself about what she could give going forward—from both a practical and an emotional perspective. It meant asking her brother to be more transparent with her. It meant asking other members of her family to step up so that she wouldn't have to manage this by herself.

Her whole life, Stacy's been the responsible one in her family. No one offers to help because they expect her to handle it, and so she does, and the cycle continues, and she's exhausted. She can't take on this role anymore, at least not alone.

A month later she sees a missed call from her brother. He only ever reaches out when he needs money, so she knows what's coming. Even though she just woke up, she notices an urge to respond—to fix it. But she was about to go for a run, so she sets her phone down and puts her needs first. After her workout, she calls her brother back and—no surprise—he askes her for money. She takes a deep breath and quietly reminds herself that she is allowed to set limits, and stays firm about the amount she's decided she can give him. She wants to help him, and this is how she can. She feels anxious about telling him what she can give, because she knows it'll disappoint him. (It's never enough.) "I know you were hoping for more, but this is all I can afford to give right now," she says to him kindly. She validates the anxiety swirling in her chest: *This is anxiety. I'm doing enough.* She feels the urge to lecture him for the hundredth time, to tell him that he needs to be better about budgeting, but she's told him this before. It doesn't get through to him, and trying to make him understand only makes her angrier. She takes another deep breath and reminds herself that she's given him what she is able to, that it is enough. She still feels waves of anxiety, guilt, and anger, but they pass through her and this interaction doesn't derail her whole day the way it would have in the past.

Leaning back from the role she's played since childhood isn't easy. For Stacy, changing her own behavior feels exhausting at first, because she has to constantly resist the urge to do what she's always done. Now she must sit with the discomfort of doing less, of doing nothing, of not knowing the outcome, of taking a new path that has historically felt dangerous. Yet Stacy knows that the alternative—continuing to play this parental role for the rest of her life—is no longer an option for her body. The way she approached this interaction worked this time, and she knows that her needs and capabilities may change in the future. She may need to reevaluate their relationship moving forward, and while it's uncomfortable, it's empowering to remember that she can change her mind.

When we fawn but call it empathy, it becomes a fast track to resenting any and all relationships that ask something of us. Empathy without boundaries can easily become self-betrayal. We can have empathy for someone while also protecting ourselves and recognizing our needs. We can understand why someone is acting the way they are and have empathy for the pain and trauma they've been through while not tolerating it. We can appreciate someone's apology and also decide that we don't want to continue a relationship with that person. **Empathy doesn't mean overextending ourselves; it means acting out of sustainable compassion.** I believe that when we're truly connected to ourselves, love, not fear, is our natural state. Healing returns us to our natural way of being. So healing the fawn response only brings us closer to *more* love and acting from love in a true, genuine way.

The Power of Resentment

Resentment is the most important emotion to pay attention to when we're beginning our boundary-setting journey. Notice when you start having fake arguments in your head. That's a sign that there is a need that isn't being met or that something needs to be acknowledged, either within yourself or with the other person. When you feel resentment in your body, you can use NICER to notice it, invite it to stay, get curious about it, and embrace it by allowing what's there to be there. In this self-inquiry, you can ask yourself these questions:

- What triggered this resentment?
- Is there a need of mine that isn't being met here?
- What boundary would I want to set in this situation if I wasn't fearful of disappointing this person?
- What boundary *can* I set in this situation, given the circumstances?

What a Boundary Is and Isn't

A boundary isn't an attempt to control the other person's behavior or to make them change. A boundary doesn't require the other person to do anything. A boundary is something you set for yourself, not for the other person. You're deciding what *you* will do, not what the other person will do. Instead of "Don't talk to me that way," a boundary could sound like "I will finish this conversation with you when you aren't raising your voice" or "If you raise your voice while we're having this conversation, I'm going to leave the room."

Instead of "Stop calling me while I'm at work," a boundary could sound like "I just wanted to let you know that if you call me while I'm at work, I won't be able to call you back until my lunch break" or "I can't answer your calls during work because I need to focus."

Setting a boundary is really just letting the other person know "This is who I am, this is what I'm about, and this is what I'm able to do."

The purpose of setting a boundary is to feel more peace within ourselves—not to avoid conflict with other people, and not to exert control over others.

Boundaries are hard to talk about in general terms because every relationship, context, and culture is going to have different kinds of boundaries. The way you can set boundaries at work is probably going to be different from the way you can set boundaries with your friends. The culture you and your family are a part of is going to influence the extent of the boundaries you can set. Because every context is different, the practice of setting boundaries requires you to pay attention to what's happening internally, knowing that only *you* can know what boundary is possible for yourself in any given scenario. The very process of deciding what boundaries are appropriate and possible *is* you healing the fawn response, because it's forcing you to look inward and trust yourself about what to say or do as opposed to looking outside yourself for guidance.

Here are the three major components of setting and keeping a boundary:

1. IDENTIFY WHAT YOU'RE FEELING AND NEEDING (internal)

Pause and look inward. Ask yourself: *What emotion is coming up for me right now? If it were up to me, what would I want to do? And now, what's possible given the context of this relationship?*

2. COMMUNICATE AND EXPRESS THAT NEED (external)

Express yourself in a way that feels authentic to you. Practice being clear and concise, and resist the urge to use fluffy or fawny language (e.g., "Is that okay with you? No worries if not!" "Sorry for existing!" "I am such a burden!").

3. MAINTAIN THE BOUNDARY (both internal and external)

When the same situation pops up again, assuming you still feel the same way, maintain the boundary and be consistent with it.

Accept That They Might Not Like It

If someone doesn't have the ability to set their own boundaries, they're going to feel agitated by *your* boundaries. That's okay. People will respect and understand your boundaries as much as they can respect their own. You're not responsible for managing their emotions, nor is doing that even in your control. You can't control other people's reactions to your boundaries. You can't force someone to change if they aren't ready to. All you can control is your own responses, your boundaries, and whom you spend your time with.

Beginning to identify and honor your needs is going to feel uncomfortable. That's normal, and it makes sense. But the fact that doing this is hard and uncomfortable doesn't mean you're doing something wrong. Each time you honor your needs and realize that you're still safe (even if someone is disappointed, you can still be safe), you're showing your body counterevidence; you're proving to the scared, protective part of you that you don't need to fear this situation as much anymore.

Someone resisting your boundary isn't a sign that you've failed at setting that boundary. Being able to tolerate the discomfort of disappointing someone is part of what makes it a successful boundary. People who think your boundaries are selfish or who push back against them are probably people who don't know how to set and respect their own boundaries and were intending to cross yours. They can certainly communicate to you how they're feeling, and that sharing can open up a discussion, but their discomfort is not something for you to fix.

Consistency Is Key

The most important part of any boundary, in whatever context or relationship, is the third step: maintaining it. I recently heard someone say, "Maintaining boundaries doesn't cause outcomes; maintaining boundaries can hasten outcomes," meaning our consistency with our boundaries simply reveals what's been there all along in the relationship and brings us closer to that clarity.

The truth is that even if people are disappointed by our boundaries or don't understand why we're setting them, consistency is comforting. We're no different from children, who crave consistency from their caregivers. Imagine a parent says to their child each night at 7:00 p.m., "Honey, time to put away our screens. I'm going to take the remote away now so that we can begin to wind down together." The child is most likely not going to respond, "Mom, I totally understand! Thank you for being such a good parent." The child will likely groan and moan and plead for five more minutes, but when the parent is consistent in maintaining the boundary, they effectively tell the child: "I'm stable, secure, and steady. You are safe with me. I'm not emotionally unpredictable." And the parent goes into the situation prepared to tolerate the discomfort of the child not loving the boundary: "I know, sweetie, I get it. It's not fun to stop doing something that brings us joy. But it's time for us to get ready for bed."

It feels good to know who the other person is and what to expect from them. This doesn't mean that you can't change your mind. This doesn't mean that just because you said no to plans one night, you need to say no to plans every night for the sake of being consistent. It means you understand what you need and what you're feeling. Your ability to communicate clearly, honestly, and directly remains consistent even as your feelings fluctuate and your decisions change depending on your internal state. When you're consistent and direct within your relationships, there may be more short-term discomfort, but there's less long-term anxiety and tension because everyone knows where they stand.

Boundaries Are a
Bid for Connection

Lauren had recently graduated from college and moved to a new state, and she was trying to navigate the world as a young adult. She was struggling to find a balance between cultivating new relationships and maintaining old relationships in her hometown—as well as manage everything else that comes with trying to build a life for yourself.

But the biggest source of conflict in her new life came from her mother.

As Lauren was adjusting to her full and busy life on her own, she felt resistance and pressure from her mom. This came up especially around holidays.

Lauren had decided that she was going to go home for Christmas, but not for Thanksgiving. The flights were too expensive, and two trips would have been exhausting since she was working full-time and couldn't take much time off around the holidays. Lauren shared her plans, along with her own disappointment, and her mom reacted with passive aggression: "Well, I guess being home is just the *worst* thing ever."

Lauren became frustrated. She felt like her mom was misunderstanding her and that what she was doing (flying home for Christmas) wasn't enough.

In this new season of her life, Lauren was telling her mom what she had the capacity for. She genuinely wanted to go home for

Christmas, but she knew that if she flew home for both holidays, it would be too much and she'd feel resentful. Going home for Christmas was her way of showing her mom: "I want to see you and am excited to see you, and this is what works this year."

Yet Lauren's mom was holding on to the expectation that their childhood holiday traditions would continue into Lauren's adulthood. She felt like her daughter's plan meant that Lauren didn't want to go home, or didn't love her, or something was wrong between them.

Mom was disappointed. Lauren was frustrated. They were both unhappy and resentful.

The miscommunication concerned the motive for the boundary. When Mom realized that Lauren was being honest and not avoiding her, she was able to release some of her expectations and respect Lauren's needs. In turn, Lauren became less defensive and felt reassured that what she was able to give was enough.

When we can understand what someone's boundary represents— an expression of the other person's needs—we gain an opportunity for more closeness, more understanding, and less resentment.

"No" Is an Opening

"The *birthday parties*. Why didn't anyone warn me about the number of birthday parties you need to go to when you have kids?" Naomi shakes her head, face in her palms as she prepares for four weekends in a row of her kids' classmates' birthday parties.

"Why were all their classmates born in September?"

"What would happen if you didn't go to *all* of them?" I ask her.

She lifts her face out of her hands and peers up at me. "I can do that?"

How often does it happen that someone asks you to do something and your body feels an immediate, visceral *ugh*? You grapple with the guilt of maybe saying no, you brainstorm potential excuses (read: white lies) that could give you an easy out, or maybe you just go anyway, begrudgingly. (Speaking of white lies, being dishonest as an attempt to set a boundary in a healthy relationship is exhausting, because you need to keep track of your white lies.)

> I want you to add "no" to your vocabulary. On the other side of "no" is the ability to trust yourself. On the other side of "no" is a life that feels good to *you*.

That's what Naomi ended up doing. She spoke with her partner, and they were on the same page: they missed their family. With all their weekend commitments, they felt far from one another, and they needed some quiet quality time as a family of four to feel close again. There was the guilt (*Am I a bad mom for not going to all of these events?*), followed by the realization that the most important thing for Naomi's family was their own well-being. By overextending herself and her family and feeling resentful, she wasn't doing her family any favors. By going to *some* of the birthday parties and not *all*—and walking her kids through that decision—she was modeling for them: *It's okay to have healthy boundaries. When we feel depleted and allow ourselves to say no to something, we open up the opportunity for something else.* In this case, more family time, more closeness.

SHOULD I GO?

We can practice feeling our noes and yeses from the neck down. The body doesn't know the difference between an imagined scenario and an actual experience, so close your eyes and visualize in as much detail as possible what the different options would look like, and therefore *feel* like, to the body. Does this option spark joy, or does it make you feel dread? Does it create tension in your body or ease?

We'll explore in the next chapter how it's helpful to release the belief that there's a "right" and a "wrong" decision—it's just a decision in which each option will lead to a different experience.

Staying True to You

"It's brutal out there," Elle says.

She's in her late twenties and is looking for love, a long-term partner and best friend whom she can feel safe with. In her past relationships and situationships, she found herself bending over backward to meet each guy's needs, saying she liked rock music even though it gave her a headache, saying she liked mozzarella sticks even though she's lactose intolerant. Same thing with sex: the guy took the lead, and she rarely stopped to consider what she wanted, what felt good to her. She thought, *If I can just be what he wants, maybe he'll stay.*

And now she's tired of it. In our work together, Elle has realized that she actually hates sleeping with people on the first date. Because she's looking for a life partner and for someone who respects what she wants, she realizes that being firm is actually a way to gather information, to determine: *Will this person respect me and my body?*

Elle went on a date last weekend, and the guy hit her with the familiar "Oh, come *on . . .*"

"In the past, I think I would've let my boundaries slip because I just wanted to be wanted. But I remembered what you said: *Would my future husband do this?* And no, he wouldn't. My future husband wouldn't guilt-trip me into intimacy. Thank you: Next!" she says.

Boundaries aren't just about canceling Friday night plans. They're about regaining sovereignty over your own life: your time, your money, your energy, your body. In order to do that, you have to know what your needs, values, and priorities are and stay true to them.

Learning to "Lean Back"

As much as we're practicing boundary setting with other people, we're also doing it with ourselves.

I worked with a client, Lydia, who was the only woman on her team at work. Each week at their team-wide meeting, someone would ask for a volunteer to take notes and the room would go quiet. Lydia would reluctantly raise her hand and scribble down the words from her colleagues, seething with resentment. This feeling came up in her personal life, too. She felt pressure to take incoming calls even if she was in the middle of something important because she didn't want anyone to have to wait and possibly get mad at her. She'd find herself texting people she didn't really care about hanging out with because she was scared they'd lose interest in her if she didn't and then she'd feel abandoned.

In our work together, we talked about the practice of what I like to call "leaning back." It's a subtle internal shift; other people may not even notice it. In areas where you normally overextend yourself, volunteer yourself, try to prove yourself *when you don't need to*—lean back. Slow down and ask yourself: *Why am I about to do this thing?* Leaning back doesn't mean you're neglecting responsibilities; it just means you're not exerting energy when you don't need to. You're leaning back, not leaving the room.

Lydia stopped being the first to volunteer to take notes, and it pushed her male colleagues to step up. She started releasing the feeling of urgency about responding to texts and phone calls and realized that no one minded or even noticed when she didn't respond right away. What Lydia discovered was that her version of "leaning back" was actually her just exerting the same amount of effort, if not more, as the people in her life. If you're a fawner,

I have a feeling your version of "leaning back" means you're still doing plenty.

With fawners, doing isn't the problem—it's *being*.

Guilty of Trying Something New

As we discussed in chapter 5, guilt tells us when we're behaving out of alignment with our personal values or standards. It's like if you get snappy with the customer service agent and then feel guilty because it goes against your values to treat someone that way, especially someone who's trying their best to help you. This is guilt, and it's appropriate here. Guilt is a useful emotion that invites us to reflect: *Why did I react that way? What led me to that point, and how can I work on managing my reactions?*

Boundary guilt is a little different. As a fawner, you have a tendency to see other people's distress or discomfort and instantaneously take it on yourself. You say to your friends, "I'm not drinking tonight," and they're disappointed and try to change your mind, and you feel guilty: *Am I ruining their night? Am I lame?* Or your volatile parent raises their voice at you, and you tell them you're going to end the call if they keep yelling, but your parent gets more reactive, and then you start beating yourself up for it: *They're upset. Was I being mean?* When we put up a boundary and stay true to ourselves and other people have a reaction to it, this will *feel* like guilt—but is it? Are you behaving out of alignment with your personal values?

When a boundary is new, or even when it's not, what sometimes follows is the feeling of immediate guilt. *This is normal.* The presence of guilt isn't a sign that you're doing something wrong; it's a sign that you're doing something new.

You think, *There's that scared, younger, protective part working so hard to keep me safe. Hello there; thank you for trying to help me. But look, I just set this boundary and nothing bad happened; I am still here and we are still safe. I can simply notice the guilt as it arises, and I can survive its temporary discomfort.*

Either way, there's something unpleasant to feel. Would you rather endure the short-term discomfort of setting a boundary or the long-term burning resentment of swallowing your needs?

When a Boundary Isn't an Option

There are certain relationships and contexts in which boundaries are inevitably harder to set. I'm sure you'd sometimes love to say "I don't have the capacity for that right now" to your boss, but that's not always the right move for your job security. Setting boundaries isn't being unrealistic or deciding we can do whatever we want, whenever we want. There's a fine line between maintaining social norms and having a fawn response. A question to return to is: *What's really necessary here?*

Say you have a coworker who grinds your gears and you don't really care about having a relationship with them outside of work, but they ask you to have lunch with them nearly every single day. You force out a "Sure!" every time they approach your desk because you do need to keep up a relationship with them, but does it have to be this much? Maybe a boundary here would look like putting lunch with them on the calendar once a week or once every other week. Ask yourself: *What do I really need to be doing here, and what's coming from an unnecessary place of fawning?*

When you aren't able to set a boundary the way you'd ideally like to, you can still use NICER to acknowledge what you're feeling, even if you can't outwardly express your feelings in the moment.

Let's say your boss sent you a super-passive-aggressive email and cc'd your boss's boss. You feel trapped. You accidentally sent the wrong due date for an upcoming project, and now your boss has corrected you in a tone that makes you want to book a one-way ticket to a faraway place where there's no trace of humanity or Wi-Fi: "Just so we're on the same page, let's confirm the current year, okay? Just want to make sure we're looking at the same calendar...." There's nothing you can say or do—you just need to go along with it—but while sitting at your desk, you let yourself pause and **N**otice what's coming up for you. You take your fingers off your keyboard and just **I**nvite what you're feeling to stay: *This is allowed to be here.* You get **C**urious about it: *What is this, what am I feeling right now?*

Is this anger? Shame? Fear? It's shame, you notice. You feel ashamed for being publicly called out, and your fear of getting in trouble is in overdrive: *Okay, this is shame.* Even though there's nothing you can do about it at the moment, you allow yourself to Embrace the shame and silently say to it, *It's okay, shame. You're safe. This is uncomfortable, but it isn't dangerous.* You then Return to what's real and true right now: the sensation of your breath in your belly, the fact that you currently have a job and didn't actually just get fired.

The purpose of this process isn't to "fix" the shame or to erase it but to allow it to be there so it doesn't get shoved away and ignored, only to build up again and again in your body.

Start Safe and Small

At this point, you understand that when we do anything new, it's going to feel terrifying simply because it's unfamiliar. This is why it's crucial to go slowly and in small steps, so that each step feels *uncomfortable* but not *unsafe* to our bodies.

In this journey of practicing being honest, saying no, and setting boundaries, it's so important to start expressing your needs to the people you feel closest to and safest with. Start with situations that feel low-stakes, whatever that means to you. That could include telling your best friend that you have only thirty minutes to chat, telling your partner that you're craving some quality one-on-one time with them; telling your best friend at work that you

253

don't want to go out for lunch every day at the mediocre salad bar around the corner because you're trying to cut back on spending.

These low-stakes situations can also include speaking up for yourself where doing so is appropriate and expected. For instance, if a restaurant accidentally messes up your order, kindly let them know so they can correct it. If your therapist isn't being as directive as you'd like them to be, provide them with feedback and ask for more guidance. If you're receiving a service, like a massage, and you're wanting more or less pressure, say so. In other words, you can take the opportunity to practice identifying your needs and advocating for them in situations in which giving feedback is not only normal but expected.

Each time you do this, you're showing the scared part of you that you can speak up for your needs and still be safe, and you're rebuilding your self-trust in the process. The more you practice speaking up, the more self-trust you'll gain and the easier expressing your needs will get.

REFLECTION QUESTIONS

1. In what ways did you learn that in order to receive love, you always needed to give more and overextend yourself?

2. Is there an area or a relationship in your life that you feel resentment about? What need of yours isn't being met?

3. What would it look like to practice boundary setting in this area or relationship?

I honor my needs and communicate them with compassion. I am not responsible for managing other people's emotions.

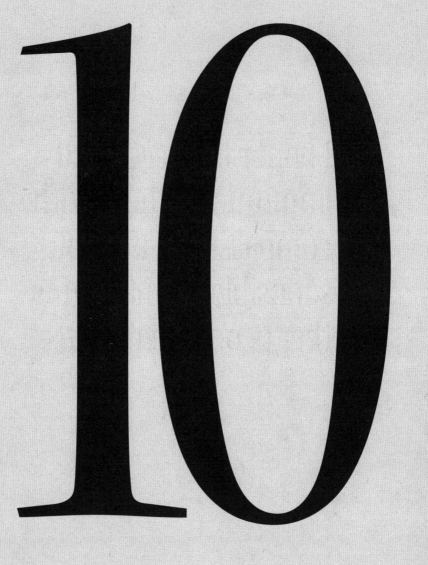

CHAPTER

10

Who Are You? (Yes, You)

*Getting to know the person
you've lost touch with*

I Don't Know Who I Am

At a school-wide assembly during my senior year of high school, a few of my classmates and I were asked to share what we'd learned about ourselves over the past few years. Most of my classmates publicly declared their lifelong aspirations in their speeches, like how they knew they were going to be a geologist from the ripe age of four and a half. Teachers shifted in the squeaky wooden pews as I rambled on about how I sometimes felt fleeting sparks of passion but didn't know if I had *one* thing that I was destined to do.

For the record, I still stand by my seventeen-year-old self. You go, girl! The idea that we're supposed to follow a single path for the rest of our lives is antiquated. Yet my refusal to plant a flag or claim an interest at seventeen didn't stem from maturity or an understanding of how much I still had to learn. It was because I was completely disconnected from myself.

If you have been stuck in the fawn response from an early age, it's normal to feel behind in life or to feel like you're meeting yourself only now, as an adult, because others your age were able to develop and explore while you were surviving and pleasing others. If you grew up pleasing a critical, controlling, or emotionally immature caregiver, their needs probably left little space for you to explore what you loved to do. If you learned from an early age that your job was to make everyone else happy—if you learned that doing what made *you* happy made other people upset and that felt unsafe—you likely shoved some of your interests aside and did whatever your caregivers wanted you to do, or whatever would garner you the most approval and acceptance from society in general. If you continue with this pattern, you might never get the chance to meet yourself.

Not knowing ourselves is such an underrecognized effect of fawning because it's so easy to hide. There's a privacy, a secrecy, to feeling lost and disconnected. If you're on the path that society deems "good," then no one will notice if you're suffering in silence. So many people don't realize they have been fawning, because it *worked*. They achieved "success." And then the cycle continues.

> No matter what age you are, it's never too late to to reestablish a relationship with your true self.

Self-Trust

I spent my twenties putting therapists, teachers, and spiritual gurus on pedestals, thinking if I just searched hard enough, I'd find the person with the golden key. They'd take one look at me and know what was wrong with me. My suffering would evaporate, I'd never get a pimple again, and everything would make sense.

It took me nearly ten years to realize that the wisdom I was seeking from others was simply uncovering what I had forgotten myself. I had prioritized everyone else's opinions of me over my own, and what I now know is that I can trust myself. I can trust that there are no secrets to uncover—clarity arises on its own through paying attention to and honoring what's happening internally. Life is not a problem to be solved or figured out; it's meant to be experienced. I no longer need to rely on external approval to guide my decisions. It's safe to listen to my inner voice.

For fawners, the need to look outside ourselves to know if we're good enough is now reinforced by the digital world. On social media, we post our lives, and our faces, and ourselves, and we say, "I'll show you who I am and you tell me if it's good enough." We look outward before looking inward. We ask others before asking ourselves. The more you heal, the less external validation you'll seek, because you'll no longer need others to tell you that your existence is good enough: you'll feel it yourself.

The practice of reconnecting with ourselves after years of fawning involves slowly building up our ability to trust ourselves. It's exploring questions like these:

- Who am I when I'm not being perceived?
- What is my personality when I'm not trying to impress or please anyone else?
- What would I want for my life if I couldn't tell anyone about it, if it wasn't being judged by others?

The "Perfect Me" Fantasy

When I decided to go to graduate school, I found myself wanting to jump ahead: *I just need to get through grad school, and then my life can start*, I thought, as if these next few years were something I had to swallow instead of savor, rush through instead of relish. The mind does this: it convinces us that once X event happens, *then* life can begin, *then* we'll be happy with ourselves, *then* we can be present and find pockets of joy.

Okay, I bargained with the inner voice. *But then you're going to tell me that my life can start once I'm a licensed therapist. And then I'll be thirty, and then you'll come up with something else to delay presence, like that I need to buy a house or pop out a kid, and* then *I'll be enough.*

The mind's tendency to create a fantasy in which everything will finally be perfect starts in our early years. In her book *Adult Children of Emotionally Immature Parents*, psychologist Lindsay Gibson describes it as a "healing fantasy."[1] In the absence of a deep, consistent emotional connection with their caregivers, children will often create a romantic, hopeful story in which their unhappiness, loneliness, and pain are cured. It usually involves changing themselves to become enough for their parents. *If I were more attractive, smarter, more athletic, then my parents would care more about me and I would feel close to them.* Often these healing fantasies are more externalized, involving imagining fame or wealth that would provide the attention and unconditional love that are missing. These fantasies are not *bad*; they're protective, and they serve a helpful function in allowing a child to escape via another reality.

As we grow into adults, we often unconsciously hold on to these fantasies and expect them to come true. We may unconsciously believe that if we were to become rich or famous or powerful or more attractive or otherwise different, then people would give us the care that we've always longed for. Or we believe that if we find or are saved by the "perfect" partner, they'll cure our lifelong emotional loneliness. When the mind is clinging to a healing fantasy, we can ask, *What is missing from my present reality that this fantasy is giving me?*

The mind's constant craving for more doesn't mean that we shouldn't strive to make our present better for the benefit of our future selves. It means doing that while also taking in what's happening now.

We're not waiting for life to start; it's here. It's this. It's accepting ourselves as we are now.

The Cost of Perfectionism

Julia's journal is where ideas go to die, she tells me. By day she works at a start-up helping someone else's idea come to life, and by night she's brainstorming ideas for her own creative endeavors, only to end them before they've begun.

"There's so much I want to say and share and create, and then I get so overwhelmed by it, I end up just doing nothing," she tells me.

If she doesn't try, there's no pressure, she can't fail, and she can't be seen as imperfect. Fear gives us so many illusions, particularly that we're better-off comfortable in our misery.

By burying her ideas further into the pages of her journal, Julia doesn't need to feel her own discomfort. She's protecting herself from the harsh inner critic and the uncomfortable sensations that go with doing something new.

Perfectionism is the enemy of self-discovery.

Remember that behind perfectionism is a part of you that is terrified of being seen, perceived, criticized, and rejected, as well as terrified of letting someone down or being seen as anything but perfect.

The scared voice can be so confusing to work with because it'll come up with any and every reason *not* to do something, to the point where it can make you feel unsure of what you want in the first place. To understand whether you're acting from a place of fear, ask yourself: *If the best-case scenario were to work out—if the worst case didn't happen—would I want it?*

Anxiety Versus Intuition

I met my husband in college, when we were both nineteen. One of my dear friends introduced us; we shook hands and chatted for a few minutes. I went back to my dorm room, called my mom, and said, "I just met my husband." Not kidding. It's a cute story only because it turned out to be true.

From the very beginning, my husband had this inexplicable safety and steadiness to him, and it was a quality that I had never experienced before in a person. The feeling of home that I had longed for my whole life, the feeling of home that I had never felt in any place but had only ever felt within myself, I felt in him. And in the ten years we've been together, he's never yelled at me, manipulated me, made me feel unsafe, or treated me as anything less than his equal. Having met him when I was so young, I was in disbelief that this feeling was possible with another person, and I was in disbelief that I deserved it. I thought that to deserve healthy love, I needed to hide in a room until I was "perfectly healed."

Nothing reveals unprocessed trauma like a new relationship. The little voice in my head was spewing out thoughts like *He's going to cheat on you. You're too damaged for him. Don't trust him. He's going to flip into a version of himself that you can't see—just you wait.*

This was the first time in my life that I was able to recognize an intuitive voice within me (*This person is safe and so are you*) and an anxious voice within me (*Fucking run!!! Trust no one!*). Maybe I was able to recognize this then because of how discordant the voices were; I had never felt so sure of something, yet the voice within me had never been so scared.

I didn't want the anxious voice to call the shots and ruin this relationship. At night I would sit on my bed, leaning against the wall on which hung an Urban Outfitters tapestry that was 100 percent a fire hazard, and journal pages and pages of anxious thoughts, letting myself see the fear from a distance. Even though I wasn't formally meditating at this point, journaling felt like my introduction to cultivating awareness of this part of myself. This was me seeing for the first time that I could be feeling fear and that didn't mean the fearful thoughts were true.

He felt safe to me, and that felt unsafe because it was entirely unfamiliar. Intuition is always available to us, waiting to be uncovered. My intuition at this point was just a dim flame nearly being smothered by the fearful part of me. But it was still there. I don't think intuition is "built"; I think it's our innate nature, already there, just beneath the surface.

"Okay, so how do I listen to my intuition?" is a question I often hear. But accessing our intuition doesn't require us to try harder; it invites us to slow down, lean back, and listen. It starts with returning to the now. Accessing our intuition is no different from receiving a package that requires a signature: you have to be here, in your home, in your body, to receive it. If you're not, you may miss it.

Distinguishing fear from intuition isn't easy. I find it helpful to focus less on what the thought is and more on how it feels. Anxiety feels jittery, tense; there's a sense of urgency to it. Intuition feels calm, clear, concise. Even if the intuitive decision is a hard decision, there's still a sense of clarity around it. Because fawning has taught us to disconnect from our intuition as a means of safety, it takes time to uncover the intuitive voice that's there. But it *is* there. The more we practice distinguishing between fear and intuition, the easier it gets to trust ourselves. It's never too late to connect to our inner world, to rekindle the flame that's been suffocated, because as long as we're alive, so is our intuition.

Give Yourself Permission to Keep Changing

At the peak of my fawning, I thought for sure I knew who I was, and that's how I now know I didn't. I thought I needed to be the final, most evolved version of myself *now*, because if I wasn't, that would mean I wasn't perfect, and that felt terrifying. I thought I needed to know everything and people needed to know that I knew everything. I thought being caught in the messy middle instead of having a neatly packaged nugget of wisdom for every situation meant that I was unraveling. I was so set on having a fixed version of myself to cling to so I could say, "This is who I am."

When we feel safe, we can spend less energy analyzing who that carefully constructed version of ourselves is—and less energy analyzing how other people are perceiving us.

We are always changing. Knowing ourselves doesn't mean we must be attached to who we think we are in this moment. With time, your body is going to change, and that's okay. You're allowed to change your mind, your beliefs, what you're needing, and how you're feeling. When we hold tight to aspects of ourselves that are inherently fleeting, we're keeping ourselves from evolving. Who you are isn't fixed. Maybe yesterday you felt quieter, needing to protect your energy from the outside world, and maybe today you feel a burst of energy, a craving to be surrounded by people. Maybe yesterday you were feeling a wave of self-doubt and were quick to label yourself "an insecure person." By attaching that label to yourself, by saying "This is who I am," you're closing yourself off from the possibility that you can change, that feelings and thoughts fluctuate when you allow them to.

Shedding

The last time I had a drink was when I was twenty-three. Initially I stopped drinking because I noticed that my postconcussive symptoms—brain fog, headaches, fatigue—got worse when I drank. My reason for continuing to abstain was emotional and spiritual. I was changing, my interests and priorities were changing, and drinking no longer fit into my life.

So much of the work I was doing internally was bringing me closer to myself, and I realized that I had been drawn to alcohol to escape myself. So I stopped drinking, and though I didn't have the intention of stopping forever, I haven't had a drink since, and I really don't see myself going back to drinking. And while I wouldn't say I struggled with addiction, I could easily see an alternate reality in which I could have.

Beautiful things unfold when you unconditionally accept the rare, strange person that you are. When you get clarity on what you want, don't be surprised when habits, people, and situations that aren't meant for you depart from your life.

Prioritize Quality Alone Time

One of the most potent things you can do to cultivate a deeper relationship with yourself is prioritize spending intentional, quality time alone. Quality alone time doesn't have to be a big thing—it can be just a few minutes of connection, fluctuating based on what season of life you're in. If you have young kids, maybe you can budget only the occasional five minutes alone. If you have more free time in your life right now, maybe you can allocate a Sunday afternoon to yourself. Your alone time can be a few minutes of sitting quietly in the waiting area before your doctor's appointment, when you'd usually burn time on your phone to keep yourself occupied. Can you allow yourself brief pockets of time to sit without distraction, without extra noise? There's no standard for what's "enough"; it's just about making it work for you and letting whatever you can do suffice.

There's freedom in giving yourself pockets of time not to consume excess information, not to go on social media, not to listen to a podcast or check your email, but to allow your energetic channel to be clear of noise so that you can hear the whisper of your own inner voice. Give yourself space. Our brains aren't supposed to be taking in that much information about ourselves and other people.

It's in these pockets of quiet alone time that I've had creative ideas pop into my conscious mind that have altered the course of my career, that I've felt an inexplicable connection to everything around me, as if barriers between my skin and the air I am breathing didn't exist.

As someone who skews toward hyperindependence, I'm no stranger to alone time, but this type of alone time is different, because in it I'm fully with myself, not neglecting myself. Hyperindependence is being emotionally lonely but pushing connection away. It's when we *want* emotional intimacy but fear having it. Loneliness is different from solitude. Being an eternal Lone Wolf can be limiting for our growth and can keep us from meeting parts of ourselves that we've learned to hide. With fawning, we unconsciously believe in two extremes: either we need to abandon ourselves to feel at home in the world or we need to abandon the world to feel at home within ourselves. True, deep healing happens when we can widen our capacity to be at home within ourselves, in our relationships, and in the world, all at the same time.

Healing hyperindependence doesn't mean we're swinging to the opposite side of the pendulum and *only* surrounding ourselves with people every second of the day; it means being connected to what we're really, truly in need of and balancing quality alone time with emotionally intimate relationships that feel nurturing and not draining. Having quality alone time doesn't preclude cultivating relationships with others—the two things feed into each other, because they both invite us to be at home within ourselves.

Ironically, it's in quality alone time that I've realized I don't want to hide myself away from emotional closeness with others. Yes, being overly self-sufficient feels safe. But having deep, meaningful relationships in which I'm allowed to show up with the messy parts of myself feels better. In mourning the familial relationships I'll never have, my heart's been cracked open to let in the friends and family I *do* have. This doesn't erase the grief. Yet it's easy to overlook those who are in our support system by focusing on those who aren't there. We can put our attention on those who are present with us instead of on those who can't be what we need.

Quality alone time could look like going for a walk or, even better, going for a walk in nature if it's accessible to you. Let yourself listen to the sounds around you. Let yourself be with whatever thoughts float into your mind and anchor yourself in your environment with your senses. Notice what you hear: birds singing, cars driving by. Notice the feeling of your feet on the ground. When your mind gets lost in stories, that's okay: just come back to now when you can. It could also look like slowing down at home, taking a bath, or rolling out a mat and doing some stretching. It could look like finding a quiet place, lighting a few candles, and journaling about the future you imagine yourself living in, what it would feel like to exist in that reality. It could look like laying out a blanket in a park and letting yourself gaze up at the sky and watch clouds pass by like your thoughts.

Dusting Off
the Daydreams

If you've been stuck in the fawn response or any form of survival mode, it might feel foreign to you to daydream because you've always had to focus on getting through what's in front of you. Over the past several years I've rekindled my ability to daydream, to envision a future and a reality that feels like *me*, because I now feel safe enough in my body to imagine a life that exists past this moment. When I allow myself to daydream, I'm not attached to the details, because minds change and people change, so an exact picture of my future is a false promise. What I tap into are the *feelings* I get when I picture my future, and I treat those feelings as whispers from my intuition, reflections of my soul's deepest desires.

When you feel a twinge of envy toward someone else's reality, you can use that as an opening into a daydream of your own. Envy is information about what you desire for yourself, masked by what you fear isn't possible. What aspect of their life do you wish to cultivate more of in your own life? What about this person's life is revealing a blueprint for what your future self is desiring?

Allowing yourself to daydream is an act of connecting to your inner child, the younger part of yourself that swims in a sense of wonder and curiosity.

Think of all the energy you spend imagining the worst-case scenario. That energy is such a waste of imagination that could be used elsewhere.

Returning to Your Childhood Self

The older I get, the more I feel like I'm returning to who I was as a child. As a kid, I found the most joy in nature, reading, and other quiet activities that could evoke a feeling of home within myself. I have blurry memories of rushing to the elementary school library on a Friday afternoon after the last bell and grabbing a few books to carry me through the weekend. I would spread a picnic blanket in our front yard while my parents watched TV in the living room and stare in awe at the full moon, lost in thought about life on other planets. Alone at our kitchen table, I would do little arts and crafts projects around the holidays just because creating made me feel warm.

I lost touch with this part of me for a long time when I was fawning. Now that I've separated my sensitivity from a fawn response, it turns out there is still a sensitive person within me who finds refuge in nature and cherishes softness and quiet. So much of healing for me has meant returning to that younger version of myself who's been here all along but just needed to know it was safe to come out again.

I had been working with Carrie for two years when she expressed a similar sort of feeling. When she was a child, people would remark on how silly and free-spirited she was. In her teenage years, when her parents' relationship became increasingly tense and volatile, she felt herself hardening. She felt like she had lost her spark out of necessity, needing to be serious and mature so that she could keep her home environment together.

Now, at thirty-three, she feels herself softening again. Her jokey, quick-witted self is emerging, and she's sprinkling vibrant pops of color into her otherwise black, white, and beige wardrobe. She's indulging her love of dance and is letting go of the need to be "perfect" at it. She finds herself wanting to welcome friends over to her apartment for themed dinners, something she always wanted to do as a kid but hadn't because she was scared to invite people over and expose to them what her home life was really like.

It's funny how so much of healing and "finding ourselves" as adults is really just returning to who we were as children before society got its grip on us, before we were taught to feel shame for being ourselves, before we were taught that our needs were too much. How did you love to spend your time as a child or as a teenager? You know, *before* you were conditioned to believe that anything that didn't have a dollar value was a waste of your time. Before you were conditioned to believe that if you made jewelry, you needed to create an Etsy shop to sell it, or if you painted, you needed to sell your paintings on commission, or if you enjoyed yoga, you needed to get a teacher certification and start offering classes. What did you love to do before you were conditioned to believe that for you to do anything, you needed to be perfect at it?

Returning to ourselves isn't an effortful act; it's a practice of surrendering and listening to the curious, wonder-filled voice that exists within all of us, with no pressure or expectations.

When I find myself feeling stuck in the mundaneness of day-to-day life, I like to imagine inviting my younger self over for dinner and how it would feel for her to see where we ended up. Even if where you are right now isn't *exactly* where you want to be, what aspects of your present reality were once part of a past daydream? The purpose of this imagining isn't to force gratitude or to shove away any challenging emotions you're feeling but to see your current reality through the eyes of your past self.

Pause and Trust Yourself First

Practice not asking everyone for their opinion when making decisions.

Practice asking, *What do I think of this?* before asking someone else what they think.

Practice taking a moment to access the stillness within you before immediately seeking reassurance from someone else.

Each time you do one of these practices, you're increasing your ability to trust yourself. This isn't to say that you shouldn't ever want or need feedback from others. Pausing and looking inward first isn't meant to strengthen hyperindependence; it's meant to strengthen the relationship you have with yourself; it's a daily opportunity to get to know the person inside of you and your preferences, desires, and opinions.

You can build up self-trust and connect to your inner world in accessible, everyday ways. Self-trust is a muscle. If you were beginning to train for a marathon, you wouldn't start by running ten miles. Your body wouldn't be able to handle it. You'd start with half a mile, challenging yourself in smaller ways that had lower stakes.

Maybe you're trying on a shirt in the dressing room and, in your indecision, you want to text a photo of it to four of your friends to see if they like it. Pause and ask yourself: Do *you* like it? How do you feel in it? Would you reach for the shirt and feel excited to wear it? You might still end up asking your friends for their thoughts— that's okay. What matters is that you break the pattern of immediately seeking external validation and ask yourself what *you* think first.

You're using your inner guidance more than you probably realize. When you can begin to notice the ways in which you're already trusting yourself, you can start to see all the ways that muscle is active right now. You just aren't consciously aware of it because it's happening automatically.

How did you know what you wanted for breakfast this morning? How did you know a smoothie sounded more appealing than toast? How did you know that you wanted to listen to upbeat music instead of a heart-wrenching ballad? How did you know that you felt like going for a walk instead of a run? How did you know that you wanted to put on an extra layer of clothing before going outside?

All day long, your intuition is communicating with you.

You're Doing Enough

Chelsea was trying to decide whether she wanted to go off birth control. In our sessions, I supported her as she navigated her feelings until she landed on a decision.

"I'm mad that I can't trust myself, that I didn't just know the answer right away," she told me.

I pointed out that her ability to talk through the different options and process how they'd feel *was* her trusting herself. It was okay if it took a little bit to get there.

We may expect that if we're attuned to our intuition, the decision will be obvious, but that's not always the case. Trusting ourselves doesn't always mean that any given decision we're making is easy. The fact that a decision is *hard* doesn't mean we are making the *wrong* decision. Trusting ourselves is about being aware of what we feel aligned with, not necessarily what feels easy.

Because our bodies don't know the difference between an imagined experience and an actual one, we can close our eyes and visualize each option, imagining the details and paying attention to how it feels in our bodies. There may not be an obvious answer, but this is a small way of "trying on" different choices and noticing how our bodies are reacting to each.

When you make decisions, however big or small, you can soothe the scared part of yourself by making one of these statements:

- There's no right or wrong decision—it's just a decision.
- Whatever decision I make is going to lead me to the exact clarity that I need.
- I'm making the best decisions I can with the knowledge and awareness I currently have.
- Every step of the way, I have choices. I'm allowed to change my mind.

Each time you remember to pause and ask yourself, *What do I think of this?* you're showing the scared part of you that it's safe to trust yourself. Even if the decision results in something unfavorable or something that brings up discomfort, you can acknowledge that you're uncomfortable but still safe.

Healing is about returning home to ourselves. There's no finish line and no award we're supposed to earn (like Person Who Really Knows Themself), because we're always evolving. The importance of returning to ourselves is accepting where we are right now—and letting that be enough.

REFLECTION QUESTIONS

1. What's your current relationship to self-trust?

2. Do you have a "Perfect Me" fantasy that holds you back from life? (*Once I do X, then I can be enough.*)

3. What's a daydream that you find your mind drifting into? What is it about that daydream that is missing from your current reality?

I trust the wisdom of my intuition. I trust myself to make decisions. I trust my inner guidance.

CHAPTER

11

Healing Is an Act of Service

Time to let you go

You're Not Alone

One of the greatest gifts that being a therapist has given me is the opportunity to witness firsthand how so many of us are experiencing similar feelings—even though we feel so alone in them. I listen as clients start their stories with "This probably sounds weird" and end them with "Do any of your other clients feel that way?"

In my second month of working as a therapist a client asked me, "Why do I always think people are mad at me?" and I was teleported back to my first therapy session, back into my twenty-year-old body. I had felt such shame, wondering, *Will you think I'm crazy once you hear everything I'm about to tell you? Will you believe my experience even if others didn't? Will you think I'm as bad as I fear I am?*

Now, when I am on the receiving end of the same question, I am reminded of just how secret and private many of our inner experiences are. As humans living in an increasingly digital and disconnected world, it's easy to feel alone, to think that no one else could be feeling what we're feeling. Even vulnerability online is inherently filtered in some way, created with the knowledge that it's going to be read, viewed, and perceived. Yet despite our different backgrounds and circumstances, the emotions we tend to hide away from the world are what connect us the most.

Pain Is Self-Centered

I know I've come a long way in my trauma healing because I'm no longer so *focused* on healing all the time. In my early twenties, I went through a dense, necessary period of heavy inner work, uncovering my shadows, reading many self-help books, and learning about different patterns and how they manifested.

Now I'm focused less on active healing and more on just living. I'm practicing radical acceptance versus wondering what's "wrong" with me.

I'm no longer waiting for the next bad thing to happen, because I recognize now that everything does change.

My core beliefs have shifted away from *Everything is my fault* and closer to *Everything is working out. I am worthy of being loved. I am safe.*

I'm no longer searching for proof that I'm in danger every waking minute, no longer running around with the urgency I once did, no longer trying to control things that were never under my control. I still have bursts of those feelings, but they're no longer my default state.

Healing can feel heavy, but I feel like I can breathe now.

—

When we're living in survival mode, we're hyperfocused on ourselves. Pain is all-consuming. If you jammed your finger in the door, your wounded finger would be the center of your attention until the pain eventually subsided. When we're in pain, physical or emotional, that pain naturally centers itself in our lives. As we heal and cultivate more awareness, that pain settles, and even if it's still there in the background, pulsating like a dull ache, our awareness is strong enough to notice something else, too, at the same time we're noticing the pain.

Your Healing Supports the Collective

As we heal, we begin to have more capacity to give to others, not out of fawning—or fear—but out of compassion.

How can we speak up for the needs of others when we can't speak up for our own? How can we advocate for someone else if we can't advocate for ourselves? How can we support someone else's liberation if we can't support our own? Any work we do to liberate ourselves is also for others. Any work we do to liberate others is also for us. The writer bell hooks said it best: "The moment we choose to love we begin to move towards freedom, to act in ways that liberate ourselves and others."[1]

With every act of compassion you show toward yourself, you're creating a ripple in the collective. Each time you respond instead of react, each time you kindly set a boundary in a relationship, each time you communicate clearly and honestly, people are consciously or unconsciously noticing. The more you step into the energy of the person you want to be, the more people feel it and pick up on it, and it shows them, *This is an option. You can do this, too.*

We can support others who are stuck in a fawn response by giving them the care that the scared, protective part of them needs: slowness, compassion, and steadiness. We can invite them to look inward when their innate response is to look outward: *What do you need right now? What are you feeling? I want to hear what you think.* We can meet their urgency with an invitation to slow down, something like *There's no rush to respond* or *Why don't you sleep on it and we can check in about it tomorrow?* Most important, by being rooted in ourselves, we're modeling for the fawners that it's safe for them to be rooted in themselves, too.

Release Perfectionism in Your Healing

Let's be real. Once you put this book down, you're going to fawn when you don't need to be fawning. You're going to emotionally react instead of consciously respond. You're going to fall into an overthinking spiral and ask for reassurance that people are not mad at you. You're going to overexplain yourself and then feel embarrassed.

All this is going to happen, because you're a human being. Slipping back into an old pattern doesn't mean that you're failing. The fact that you *notice* when you fall back into the old pattern—*that* is the progress. Think about all the years you were fawning without even realizing it. Healing starts with awareness. Notice the harsh voice that views healing as another leg of perfectionism, the voice that says, *Wow, you can't even do healing right. What's wrong with you? You need to do a better job!* How you *relate* to that voice—that's the healing. Each time you insert a pause, each time you speak to that scared part of yourself with a bit more compassion, you're planting a seed for your healing, a seed that will grow and expand with time, patience, and nurturing.

You're not just healing your own patterns; you're healing generations of silenced needs and self-neglect. You're processing generations of trauma that your ancestors before you didn't have the knowledge, resources, or awareness to process themselves. You're sifting through a backlog of pain and patterns that others didn't sift through. Be easy on yourself.

Healing is a daily practice of having the courage to be with our discomfort. It's having compassion for the parts of ourselves that have been exiled. Change doesn't happen overnight. There's no measurable goal. There's just right now.

Healing myself helps to heal the collective. I am healing at the exact pace that I'm supposed to.

Acknowledgments

Just three days after turning in my final manuscript, my dad passed away suddenly and unexpectedly, due to health-related causes. It's quite confusing how, in this book, I talk so much about the slow process of grappling with my mom's mortality, yet she outlived him. I wrote this book with the careful expectation that he'd read it, and although he never will, I'm grateful for his support in me telling my story. While his presence was already deeply interwoven into parts of this book, his passing adds a certain complexity to these pages and serves as another reminder of the many messy layers of grief.

As humans, we're not meant to do everything on our own. Luckily, I've had the support of so many people in bringing this book into being, as I couldn't possibly have handled this process alone.

Rebecca Gradinger, I'll never understand how I got lucky enough to land in this wild book world with you as my literary agent. You are brilliant. Thank you for trusting me, supporting me, brainstorming with me, and dreaming with me, and for being such a reliable, steady presence. This is just the beginning!

Lauren Spiegel, my fabulous editor, your thoughtfulness, clarity, and grounded thinking are felt in these pages. Writing a book like this, let alone a *first* book like this, is a vulnerable process, and you made me feel so safe.

A huge thank-you to the fabulous team at Gallery for working so hard to launch my firstborn into the world so smoothly. Jen Bergstrom, thank you for your brilliance, enthusiasm, and zest. Thank you to Aimée Bell, Sally Marvin, Jen Long, Lisa Litwack, Jill Siegel, Lucy Nalen, Taylor Rondestvedt, Mackenzie Hickey, Fallon McKnight, Olivia Crowley, Sarah Westergren, Kimberly Laws, Caroline Pallotta, Nancy Tonik, Brigid Black, and Jon Karp.

Thank you to Rodrigo Corral for designing a timeless cover and to Kate Kenney-Peterson for a gorgeous interior design.

UTA is home to the best. Maddy Hernick, thank you for your hard work and support in the proposal process and beyond. Thank you to Ethan Schlatter, Georgie Mellor, Katie Harrison, and Melissa Chinchillo for your incredible efforts to put this book into the hands of fawners around the world. You all are rock stars!

Thank you to my lovely team across the pond, including Sabhbh Curran, my UK agent, for seamlessly bringing *Are You Mad at Me?* into the global market. Thank you to the UK team at Square Peg; Marianne Tatepo, my UK editor; and the publicity and marketing team: Mia Quibell-Smith, Amelia Rushen, and Morgan Dun-Campbell.

Thank you to my clinical supervisors from graduate school till now. I hold your wisdom in my heart—but if only I could fit it all. I still have so much to learn, and I hope I can be as fabulous a therapist one day as you all are.

To my dear friends, you know who you are. It's a special thing to feel truly known by someone.

Thank you to my brothers for your support. Thank you to my

dad for encouraging me to tell my story authentically. Mom, thank you for all the opportunities you gave me. I hope I have made you proud.

To my "bonus" in-law family, thank you for welcoming me from day one. Just by existing, you have healed so many parts of me.

H: For the past ten years, amid all of life's changes, you've been my constant. Thank you for showing me that love is safe. You invite me to dream bigger but never pressure me to. Thank you for your *I can handle dinner tonight* texts when I had to work into the night and for being my sounding board as I rambled on about ideas during our weekend walks. Your support is unwavering, and a lifetime isn't enough.

To anyone who's been a sweet supporter and community member on Instagram, TikTok, Substack, or YouTube—thank you for being here. It's a privilege to be able to share my innermost thoughts with people across the globe, and it's a responsibility that I don't take lightly.

A deep, loving thank-you to my clients, past and present. No class in graduate school could've prepared me for how special the therapeutic relationship is. Thank you for trusting me and for letting me into your worlds. I hold your stories close in my heart and will always be rooting for you.

And finally, dear reader, thank you for picking up this book, for having the courage to look at the parts of yourself that have been pushed aside, and for working hard to create a life that's liberating.

May you be free.

Notes

CHAPTER 1: THE OTHER F-WORD

1. Pete Walker, M.A., MFT, "Codependency, Trauma, and the Fawn Response," https://pete-walker.com/codependencyFawnResponse.htm.
2. W. B. Cannon, *The Wisdom of the Body* (W. W. Norton, 1932).
3. Due Quach, "The Fawn Response to Racism (Part 1): A Reflection on POC Strategies to Mitigate Violent Oppression," *Psychology Today* (April 30, 2021), https://www.psychology today.com/us/blog/healing-oppression/202104/the-fawn-response-racism.

CHAPTER 2: NOW & THEN

1. Robert R. McCrae and Paul T. Costa Jr., "Personality, Coping, and Coping Effectiveness in an Adult Sample," *Journal of Personality* 54, no. 2 (June 1986): 385–404, https://doi.org/10.1111/j.1467-6494.1986.tb00401.x.
2. Marla Paul, "How Traumatic Memories Hide in the Brain, and How to Retrieve Them," Northwestern University Feinberg School of Medicine (August 17, 2015), https://news.feinberg.northwestern.edu/2015/08/17/how-traumatic-memories-hide-in-the-brain/.
3. John Bowlby, *The Making and Breaking of Affectional Bonds* (New York: Routledge, 1979).
4. Dean V. Buonomano and Michael M. Merzenich, "Cortical Plasticity: From Synapses to Maps," *Annual Review of Neuroscience* 21 (March 1998): 149–86, https://doi.org/10.1146/annurev.neuro.21.1.149.

CHAPTER 4: YOU ARE NOT YOUR THOUGHTS

1. K. Sweeny and S. E. Andrews, "Mapping Individual Differences in the Experience of a Waiting Period," *Journal of Personality and Social Psychology* 106, no. 6 (2014): 1015–30, https://doi.org/10.1037/a0036031.
2. Melanie Klein, "The Development of a Child," *International Journal of Psychoanalysis* 4 (1920): 419–74.
3. John B. Watson, *Behaviorism* (University of Chicago Press, 1960).
4. Richard Schwartz, *No Bad Parts: Healing Trauma and Restoring Wholeness with the Internal Family Systems Model* (Sounds True, 2021).

CHAPTER 5: EMOTIONS AREN'T THE PROBLEM

1. Bessel van der Kolk, MD, *The Body Keeps the Score: Brain, Mind, and Body in the Healing of Trauma* (Viking, 2014).
2. Jaak Panksepp, *Affective Neuroscience: The Foundations of Human and Animal Emotions* (Oxford University Press, 2009).

3. Jill Bolte Taylor, PhD, *My Stroke of Insight: A Brain Scientist's Personal Journey* (New American Library, 2009).

CHAPTER 6: THIS IS EXHAUSTING

1. Aditi Nerurkar et al., "When Physicians Counsel About Stress: Results of a National Study," *JAMA Internal Medicine* 173, no. 1 (2013): 76–77, https://doi.org/10.1001/2013.jamainternmed.480.

2. DeLisa Fairweather and Noel R. Rose, "Women and Autoimmune Diseases," *Emerging Infectious Diseases* 10, no. 11 (November 2004): 2005–2011, https://doi.org/10.3201/eid1011.040367.

3. Ljudmila Stojanovich and Dragomir Marisavljevich, "Stress as a Trigger of Autoimmune Disease," *Autoimmunity Reviews* 7, no. 3 (January 2008): 209–13, https://doi.org/10.1016/j.autrev.2007.11.007.

4. George F. Solomon and Rudolf H. Moos, "The Relationship of Personality to the Presence of Rheumatoid Factor in Asymptomatic Relatives of Patients with Rheumatoid Arthritis," *Biopsycholosocial Science and Medicine* 27, no. 4 (July 1965): 350–60, https://journals.lww.com/bsam/abstract/1965/07000/the_relationship_of_personality_to_the_presence_of.6.aspx.

5. Wade W. Nobles, *African Psychology: Toward Its Reclamation, Reascension and Revitalization* (Institute for the Advanced Study of Black Family Life & Culture, 1986).

6. Brianna Chu et al., "Physiology, Stress Reaction," National Library of Medicine (updated May 7, 2024), https://www.ncbi.nlm.nih.gov/books/NBK541120/.

7. Judith Herman, *Trauma and Recovery: The Aftermath of Violence—from Domestic Abuse to Political Terror* (Basic Books, 1997).

8. Hidetaka Hamasaki, "Effects of Diaphragmatic Breathing on Health: A Narrative Review," *Medicines* 7, no. 10 (2020): 65, https://doi.org/10.3390/medicines7100065.

9. Jaak Panksepp, "Primary Process Affects and Brain Oxytocin," *Biological Psychiatry* 65, no. 9 (May 2009): 725–27, https://doi.org/10.1016/j.biopsych.2009.02.004.

10. A. H. Maslow, "A Theory of Human Motivation," *Psychological Review* 50, no. 4 (1943): 370–96, https://doi.org/10.1037/h0054346.

11. Rachel Yehuda, Sarah L. Halligan, and Linda M. Bierer, "Cortisol Levels in Adult Offspring of Holocaust Survivors: Relation to PTSD Symptom Severity in the Parent and Child," *Psychoneuroendocrinology* 27, nos. 1–2 (January–February 2002): 171–80.

12. Mariel Buqué, MD, *Break the Cycle: A Guide to Healing Intergenerational Trauma* (Dutton, 2024).

13. Sasha Lavoie, "Trauma Can Be Passed Down Through Generations," University of Calgary, September 29, 2021, https://ucalgary.ca/news/trauma-can-be-passed-down-through-generations.

14. Aiesha T. Lee et al., "Addressing Intergenerationl Trauma in Black Families: Trauma-Informed Socioculturally Attuned Family Therapy," *Journal of Marital and Family Therapy* 49, no. 2 (April 2023): https://doi.org/10.1111/jmft.12632.

CHAPTER 7: NOTHING IS PERSONAL

1. T. Gilovich, "The Spotlight Effect in Social Judgment: An Egocentric Bias in Estimates of the Salience of One's Own Actions and Appearance," *Journal of Personality and Social Psychology* 78, no. 2 (2000): 211–22, https://doi.org/10.1037/0022-3514.78.2.211.
2. T. Gilovich, V. H. Medvec, and K. Savitsky, "The Illusion of Transparency: Biased Assessments of Others' Ability to Read One's Emotional States," *Journal of Personality and Social Psychology* 75, no. 2 (1998): 332–46, https://doi.org/10.1037/0022-3514.75.2.332.

CHAPTER 9: REBRANDING BOUNDARIES

1. J. Leaviss and L. Utley, "Psychotherapeutic Benefits of Compassion-Focused Therapy: An Early Systematic Review," *Psychological Medicine* 45, no. 5 (2015): 927–45, https://doi.org/10.1017/S0033291714002141.

CHAPTER 10: WHO ARE YOU? (YES, YOU)

1. Lindsay C. Gibson, PsyD, *Adult Children of Emotionally Immature Parents: How to Heal from Distant, Rejecting, or Self-Involved Parents* (New Harbinger Publications, 2015).

CHAPTER 11: HEALING IS AN ACT OF SERVICE

1. bell hooks, *All About Love: New Visions* (William Morrow, 2000).